Effigies II

ALLISON ADELLE HEDGE COKE descends from moundbuilders and is of Cherokee, Creek, Huron, Metis, French Canadian, Lorraine, Portuguese, Irish, English, and Scot ascendants. Raised in North Carolina, the Plains and Canada, she previously worked horses, fields, waters, and factories. A fellow of the Weymouth Center for the Arts & Humanities, Black Earth Institute (emeritus), and The Center for Great Plains Institute, and Salon Ada, with recent residencies at H. J. Andrews Experimental Forest (National Science Foundation), Hawthornden Castle and Lannan at Marfa, Hedge Coke has held two endowed chairs, is field faculty for the University of Nebraska MFA Program and Naropa University and currently serves as a Visiting Writer for the University of Central Oklahoma and the University of California, Riverside. In fall, 2014, she will be the Distinguished Writer for the University of Hawaii at Manoa. Hedge Coke is a literary activist, works with disaster relief, incarcerated youth, elders, and in various alternative populations in need and founded and directs the annual Literary Sandhill Crane Retreat & Festival at the migration epicenter. She previously authored *Dog Road Woman* (American Book Award for Poetry) and *Off-Season City Pipe* (Wordcraft Writer of the Year in Poetry), both from Coffee House Press; *Rock, Ghost, Willow, Deer* (AIROS Book of the Month, paperback 2014), memoir from the University of Nebraska Press; *Blood Run* (Wordcraft Writer of the Year for Poetry) from Earthworks of Salt Publishing; and *The Year of the Rat* (Grimes Press). *Burn* (MadHat) and *Streaming* (Coffee House Press) are 2014 releases in poetry and she is currently at work on *Red Dust*, a film documentary. Recently edited anthologies include, *Effigies* and *Sing: Poetry from the Indigenous Americas* (National Book Critics Circle Critical Mass Best of 2011, Wordcraft Circle Best Editing of 2012). *Effigies II* is her ninth edited volume.

Effigies II

An Anthology of
New Indigenous Writing
Mainland North & South United States, 2014

Edited by

Allison Adelle Hedge Coke

CROMER

PUBLISHED BY SALT

12 Norwich Road, Cromer, Norfolk NR27 0AX United Kingdom

First published 2014

Printed and bound in the United States by Lightning Source Inc

Typeset in Swift 9.5 / 13

ISBN 978 1 84471 895 5 paperback

1 3 5 7 9 8 6 4 2

*This book is for every sister nation and every cousin
kinship patterning relations from tribe to tattoo.*

This book is for you.

Contents

Acknowledgements

LAURA DA'

Grateful acknowledgment is made to the editors of the following publications in which these poems appeared:

"Raven Talks Curriculum," "Spring Thaw and the Land Runs," and "Winter Dance of the Oldest Child," in *American Indian Culture and Research Journal*.
"Measuring the Distance to Oklahoma" in *Drunken Boat*.
"Basement Storage at the Museum of the American Indian" in *First Intensity*.
"Five Songs for Lazarus Shale," "The Tecumseh Motel," and "Vantage" in *Hanging Loose*.
"A Mighty Pulverizing Machine" and "American Towns" in *Mudlark*.
"Hived Bees in Winter," "No Longer," and "Wars of Attrition" in *Prairie Schooner*. Folio Editor, Sherman Alexie, for Editor Kwame Dawes.

UNGELBAH DAVILA

"Boys of Burque" published in *Catch Up* #3, 2013. Guest Editor D.A. Powell.
"Sex in the Soda Shop" published in THE Magazine, October 2012.
"The Distance of Breath," "Country Music Gave Her the Courage to Break Your Heart," and "1,000 Miles" published in American Indian Culture and Research Journal, Volume 35, Number 4, 2011.
An earlier version of "'54" titled "Bench Seats," "Looking for Monkeys by the Rio Grande," an earlier version of "In The Time of Tulips Bent Beneath Her Feet" titled "In The Time of

Tulips Bent Beneath His Window," "Tea Cup," "Smiling Shoulders at the Flying Star Café," published 2012 in *Drunken Boat #15*. Folio Editor Layli Long Soldier, for Editor Ravi Shankar.

Some versions of poems included also published in IAIA Anthologies *Voyeurs of War* and *Birds, and Other Omens*.

KRISTI LEORA

"Perimeters: Their Revolution" appeared in Fall 2011 issue of Talking
    Stick: Native Arts Quarterly published by Amerinda.
"Ascension" in 2014 issue of *Fulcrum Poetry: an anthology
    of poetry and aesthetics*, Allison Hedge Coke, folio
    editor.

LARA MANN

"Nanih Waiya Cave"
    Isaac Pistonatubbee quote is located in *Choctaw Social and
    Ceremonial Life* by John Swanton. Swanton is quoting H. S.
    Halbert's work in Publs. Miss. Hist. Soc., volume IV, pp.
    267-270, Oxford, Miss., 1901.
"Summertime Death Song"
    "*one of these mornings . . .*" quote is from George Gershwin's
    Porgy and Bess; lyrics by DuBose Heyward and Ira
    Gershwin.
"A Song of Ascents and Descents"
    "*Save me, O Lord . . .*" quote is Psalm 120:2 in the New
    International Version Study Bible. "*Faith of
    Our Fathers . . .*" quote is from the song *Faith of
        Our Fathers* by Frederick W. Faber in the Methodist
    Hymnal. "*If I have a faith . . .*" quote is from 1 Corinthians
    13:2 in the New International Version Study Bible.
"How the Great American Indian Novel is Written"
    This poem was written after, and in response to, Sherman

Alexie's "How to Write the Great American Indian Novel" from *The Summer of Black Widows*.

"Apprentice"

The Overture of Le Nozze di Figaro referenced is from *Le Nozze di Figaro (The Marriage of Figaro)* by Wolfgang Amadeus Mozart.

"In the Absence of Bone Pickers"

"*Swing Low* . . ." quote is from the song *Swing Low, Sweet Chariot*, an African American Spiritual.

"Silver Creek Sound Stage"

An earlier version of this poem appeared as "Silks" in the *Coal City Review* 21:2006.

"Grandma's Yard Art . . .," "Silver Creek Water Spider . . .," "Cousin-Kin Carnival . . .," and "Silver Creek Fruit and Stock Farm Barn . . ."

Each of these poems pairs with a piece of music, as indicated, from the Peer Gynt Suite No. 1, Op. 46 by Edvard Greig.

"Okla Humma"

published in 2005 in the Kiosk *Art and Literature Review*. Editor Ashley Puderbaugh.

"Silks"

published in 2006 in *Coal City Review*. Editor Brian Daldorph.

"Purebred Hybrid Vigor," "Felling," "Witness," and "Ball Games"

published in the Fall 2008 edition of the *Connecticut Review*. Folio Editors LeAnne Howe and Allison Hedge Coke, for Editor John Briggs.

"Apprentice"

published Fall 2008 in *Many Mountains Moving*. Folio Editor Diane Glancy, for Editors Debra Bokur and Jeffrey Ethan Lee.

"Affliction of Ritual" published 2009 in *Sentence Magazine* Volume 7. Editor Dean Rader.

"How the Great American Indian Novel is Written"

Published Summer 2010 in *Drunken Boat* #12. Editor,

Ravi Shankar. 2011. Republished in *Arcadia*, Editor Noah
Milligan.
"In the Absence of Bone Pickers
anthologized in *Sing: Poetry from the Indigenous Americas*,
University of Arizona Press, 2012. Editor Allison Hedge
Coke.
"My Ceremony For Taking," "Nanih Waiya Cave,"
"Grandma's Yard Art," and "Silver Creek Fruit and
Stock . . ."
published in *Drunken Boat* #15. Folio Editor Layli Long
Soldier, for Editor Ravi Shankar.
"Straight Line Talking"
published, 2013, in the Asian American Literary Review,
Mixed Race in a Box Edition. Folio Editors Jennifer Foerster
and Allison Hedge Coke, for Editors-in-Chief Lawrence-
Minh Bùi Davis and Gerald Maa.

KATERI MENOMINEE

"Geomancy," "Outside the Wall of Crosses," "Tectum," and "The
Ignorance of Milk" published 2012 in *Drunken Boat* #15.
Folio Editor Layli Long Soldier, for Editor Ravi Shankar.

Some versions of poems included also published in IAIA
Anthologies *Radical Enjambment*; *Birds, and Other Omens*; and
Of Water and Moon.

Editor's Note

These five new poets bear potent language, portray insightful glimpses of experiential realities and the more deeply conceived and exhibit shades of sheer grace in their debut poetics. Measured by intuitive explorations, their luminous lingual transformations lead us into a remarkable contemporary journey in these Choctaw, Dine', Anishinaabe, Onondaga and Shawnee poets' locations of thought and lives. This work is essential reading; nourishment.

It is at once a privilege and pleasure to bring these poets together to create a body of work introducing these books and the beginnings of what are sure to be brilliant careers ahead of them in the ready field.

Joining dg nanouk okpik, Cathy Tagnak Rexford, Brandy Nalani McDougall and Ma'healani Perez-Wendt, collected in the first Effigies release, Lara Mann, Ungelbah Davila, Kateri Menominee, Kristi Leora and Laura Da' contribute a remarkable array of vital verse and secure us in sweet indulgence while we witness a swiftly moving field progression with a sure fusion rarely met. This is vibrant work from five entering poets and we are the better for it and for reveling in what they bring bursting in. Synaptic.

The editor thanks each wonderful contributor and Salt Publications, Janet McAdams, LeAnne Howe, Sherwin Bitsui, Arthur Sze and Jon Davis for your part in making this collection great. Stunning work.

ALLISON ADELLE HEDGE COKE, Editor of *Effigies*
and *Sing: Poetry of the Indigenous Americas*

Laura Da'

The Tecumseh Motel

The Tecumseh Motel traces a parallel path of Shawnee culture and personal history. Spanning from the period of Indian Removal to the present, this text lyrically examines identity, generational memory, and the importance of place.

I owe a debt of gratitude and heartfelt thanks to all the people who have supported the creation of this manuscript. First, I would like to honor my husband, son, and family for their guidance, encouragement, and time. I would also like to credit the Eastern Shawnee Tribe of Oklahoma for support and inspiration. Some of these poems were written at the Institute of American Indian Arts and the Richard Hugo House in Seattle, and I appreciate the advocacy and instruction both organizations have provided me and generations of other writers. I have been inspired and encouraged for the past ten years by my students at Tyee Middle School and Highland Middle School.

Poets and friends who have provided support include: Sherman Alexie, Sherwin Bitsui, Allison Hedge Coke, Jon Davis, Tara Hardy, Mischele Jamgochian, and Arthur Sze. "Vantage" is dedicated to my son Tony.

Laura Da'

Raven Talks Curriculum

1.

Raven curls his talons
against the newspaper rag
of a seventh grade textbook
that attributes his myth
to an anthropologist
who traveled along the Pacific Coast
fifty years ago
recording tribal creation stories.

2.

In fifth grade, I rode the bus
to the local museum on a school field trip.

The river was splitting its banks,
creeping up the margins of the road.
Mottled stones
with the patchy lichen-skin
and bulky silhouettes
of kids slumped on a couch
were disappearing
under the murky slush of flood water.
Bright pink flash of molting leaves
glimpsed through the bus window
hinted at salmon in the eddy.

At the museum, I was unhinged by old bounty signs
from the fur wars

offering the largest pile of gold for men's scalps,
less for women,
a token amount for children and infants.

I traced my finger over the name Snoqualmie, unbelieving.

Listening to the curator read aloud from the myth of raven,
I counted on my fingers
back ten years at a time to 1860
until the teacher jerked them away into my lap
and snapped my attention to the front.

3.

Fifty years ago,
The five most likely
themes employed to describe
Native Americans in textbooks:
Noble Savage
Warrior
Chief
Protestor
White Man's Helper

2013: the school district procures
new texts—feigned Native narratives.
As if to say with a shrug,
colonialism had children and grand-children too.
In the end, even the stories are acquisitions.

        Who is this trickster
sauntering receding coasts
scattering light and darkness?

4.

Heavy thud of the book
slamming shut
pinions Raven into a bentwood box of pulp
where dark seeps out of the feathery ink of the font.

The students shade the standardized test
in fine, soft strokes of graphite—fish-scale dents
on the show and tell arrowhead.

The Tecumseh Motel

In Shawnee cosmology,
a shooting star can fall to earth as a mythical panther.

> Tecumseh—
> phonetic approximation of an Algonquian name:
> Shooting Star,
> One Who Waits,
> Crouching Panther.

The first cultural event in Chillicothe
is a matinee performance
of an outdoor play
highlighting Tecumseh's life.
We are honored guests,
ushered backstage before the show.

How to approximate a scalping
at the Tecumseh Outdoor Drama:
> Hollow an egg with care.
> Fill with Karo syrup and red tempera paint.
> Soak a toupee with cherry Kool-Aid
> and mineral oil.
> Crack the egg onto the actor's head.
> Red matter will slide down the crown
> and egg shell will mimic shards of skull.

Actors on horseback frame the stage.
A roan flicks his tail irritably at flies
as his rider shifts uncertainly on the saddle blanket.

How to approximate death by gauntlet:
> The victim must lead the action.
> The aggressor follows.
> Burn marks are approximated on the actor's chest
> with burnt ends of wine corks

hidden in the sand at his feet.
The knife is dull edged,
lined with a small tubing mechanism.
The actor squeezes a pump
of corn syrup, liquid soap, and red food dye
in a limp arc across the torso.

At the end of the performance
the crowd turns a standing ovation

to the representatives of our tribe
sitting in the middle rows.
Are we mocked or honored with such a display?
That evening,
I rail glibly on the telephone:
            historical inaccuracies,
                        hooping and hollering,
                                    pandering to the worst stereotypes.
My husband interrupts me—
            you sound like you've been crying.

            A Chillicothe chief to the British Army Commander
in 1779:
            We have always been the frontier.

American Towns

Seneca, Missouri—soft wash of casino jangle
seeps through the Pontiac's cracked window.

The map flutters on the dashboard,
one corner grit-soaked.

Sparse Ozark wash of tawny green.
A herd of buffalo lowing in the side pasture.

Here is the voyage,
conjured homeland to conjured homeland.

No, not that clawed trajectory of the past,
but a fierce conception

that quickens and scrapes inside just the same.
The drive to Ohio will take

eleven hours and forty-eight minutes,
cost one-hundred and ninety-five dollars in gas.

Chillicothe—in the subtle semantics
of Shawnee, a tightened fist of connotation:

clan name and principal city,
all human systems working in harmony.

Limpid sashay of corn tassels along the byway.
Historical markers beckon the reader

to plunge an arm into the loam
tweeze with fingers to feel how fecund,

no rocks to bend the ploughshare.
What heirloom fields of Shawnee

corn hum under the crust
beside the carbon of burned council houses?

August wheeze of Bad Axe Creek.
Drought thrusts large boulders jutting up waist-high,

deep grooves in the center
for grinding corn. What is owed

grits in the corners of the mouth.
The plaque on the museum's door in Xenia extols

a Revolutionary War hero:
The ground on which this council house stands is unstained

with blood and is pure as my heart which wishes
for nothing so much as peace and brotherly love.

Summer school kids mill around the museum.
The teacher introduces the panel of tribal council members

as *remnants of the once great Shawnee tribe.*
Listless murmur of pencils across paper.

In the front room, a volunteer curator leans over a diorama
anxious to capture the real story

of a Revolutionary War camp.
He stipples red paint onto the sandy ground

simulating the gore of a military flogging,
points with the paintbrush to the next room

where fifty-three letters from 1783 broker captive trades
with the Delaware and Shawnee:

wan shades of ink from blanched olive to cornflower,
blotted in the rough or refined sway of long dead hands

each one made phylum by the promise of whisky.
Leaving Xenia that evening on an old Shawnee trade route

re-traced in concrete: Monlutha's Town, Wapakoneta,
Blue Jacket's Town, Mackachack, Wapotomica.

Xenia—the influence of the pollen
upon the form of the fruit.

I want my ink to bellow—
where is this ground unstained with blood?

Five Songs for Lazarus Shale

It gives me pleasure to announce to Congress that the benevolent policy of the Government, steadily pursued for nearly thirty years, in relation to the removal of the Indians beyond the white settlement is approaching to a happy consummation.

PRESIDENT ANDREW JACKSON, 1830

1.

There was a word for village
that meant all at once:
perfect home
perfect man
all human systems working in harmony.
A Shawnee village was a good genius society.
Names were to be guarded.

First memory:
clambering onto a horse
toes splayed for purchase
peering over the swayed back
at a curving glimmer of tributaries.
Listing rows of corn as far as the eyes could travel.

2.

Running on spindly legs
and speaking in a bubbling rush of Shawnee
the boy fled through cane breaks
when the Indian Agent called.

A child's arrow tipped with a gar's fin
pointed to the eddy.

In the wilted moon,
the Quakers gave him the name.
Bible held hovering out of reach

as he grasped at the inked picture
of a man shouldering out of a stone tomb.

The agent sat in the back pew, sniffing the end of a quill,
a slim flask of ink between his knees.
Wet trail of letters on the ledger: Lazarus Shale.

   3.

Tawny coffee beans, bolts of calico, molasses,
rations passed out the back door.
Speculation at the trading post
on the topic of removal:
Lewistown first, then Lima village
Hog Creek on down the curve of the river to Wapakoneta.

Sap moon cold.
Traders walking foundered horses over coals
anticipating army requisitions.

Lazarus tracing letters in the ash,
his aunt stitching rounded meadow flowers onto doe skin:
pumpkin yellow, greasy blue and green, white-heart red
      beads.
The baby waking every so often to press a few grains into her
      chubby fingertips.
Tallow flicker across their mother.

Why Sister, you're beading in the old style.

In the rafters,
her fingers turning back to unbraiding.
The family's dried corn falling in dusty ropes.

4.

Journeying Cake.

In the morning,
Quakers pressed wrapped suppers into their hands,
reading from the Book of Ruth over the noise of the muster.

Generic native ash-cake baked in an open fire.

Dig under the crust to find the varieties of corn
in the charred fields of Wapakoneta:
dent
flint
Boone County White
Bloody Butcher

Journeying cake Shawnee cake or every man's cake becoming jonny or
*   johnny cake.*

Walking away, south along the Scioto
looking back often.
Vivid shoots of green corn
rippling along the trail in a delicate commotion.
Fingers bent against the leather satchel
pinching at grains of corn bread.
Lazarus, who else could tell this story?

5.

In Shawnee tradition
one is cautioned to cross a river
quickly, without looking down
to tempt swift creatures
ready to rend the body in riparian embrace.

Underwater panthers.
Left to ponder such beings,
the mind balks.
Mad River.
Scioto.
Great and Little Miami.

Shawnee translations of the rivers of Wapakoneta.
Auglaize River: the falling timbers on the river.
Blanchard's Ford of the Auglaize: claws in the water.

Hived Bees in Winter

The Indians (as yesterday) remained as quiet as hived bees in the winter.
DANIEL R. DUNIHUE, SUPERINTENDENT OF INDIAN REMOVAL
Journal of Occurrences, 1832

1.

Plum moon heat—deep and pungent.
The Wapakoneta band of Shawnee
muster in a grove to wait for four day's rations.

In the periphery,
the horizon is a memory palace.
A verse is woven
into the curve of the river.
Hiding in a fringed prairie opening
is an account
of the maiden
who fell in love with the loon.

Driven slowly into the west,
the old folks walk cowed
bending low into the corn.

Three men petition for permission to make camp
beside hunched burial mounds
along the Scioto.

The superintendent of Indian affairs acquiesces:
        I did intend going tonight to the feast of the Indians.
        Death feast.
Upon leaving the graves,
an orator laments.
        It is their custom to recite
        and mutually and undisquietly
        express their sorrow for their losses.

The superintendent is startled awake
by a stray horse trailing a rawhide hobble.
The heat is gentle yet.
A line of women are sitting on the wagon and chanting;
under their draped legs are sleeping children.

In the miles that follow,
a singer prods the corners of his mouth
scanning the horizon for a forgotten refrain.

2.

South of Fort Wayne,
wilted moon
sweats the Maumee River.
A woman wakes the camp
shaking and clattering her arms together.
Wet cough like a bare foot sucked out of deep mud.

Young ones
scour the fields for corn cobs
lingering after the harvest.
Their bones recognize the chill is different,
punctuated one night by a prairie fire
wafting on tall grass and crackling to the east.
Waxed comb dragged through hair,
heavy with the smell of bear grease and honey.
Crackle and snap as lice and eggs are lathed
onto a whetstone and flicked into the fire.

The horses scrape lichen from tree trunks,
grow surly and thin,
foundered in trail sludge.

Lazarus is lolling along the back of one.
Palms down on its shaggy neck
to soak up the warmth.

The superintendent calls a halt
at the intersection
of the St Joseph, St. Mary's, and the Maumee
and ponders the flooded rivers
from early morning to mid-afternoon.

Militia men place bets
and aim at a sleeping turtle on the opposite bank.

Fording in the early evening,
they cross through razed corn fields

and march down the portage road
to the Wabash Agency.
Gawkers spread around.
Shivering in the muddy space between
the quartermaster's shack
and the kitchen garden.

A man in a waxed brown cape
darts in and out of the crowd
flashing a flask and sloshing whiskey in a bottle.

Lazarus buries his face into his cousin's tunic.
With two fingers, the man twists his chin back out
into the gloaming.

   3.

December's moon is eccentric,
January's severe.

Clean geometry of trumpeter swans stitching
a slab of sky.

Snuffling bear
'on the edge of the encampment
nosing for a cache of acorns.

Lazarus has been chewing the horses' oats,
nibbling the trampled grass,
dusty tang of urine and hint of molasses on his molars.

The flock of swans
lights down and,
in their churning multitude,
they melt a frozen pond to sleet.
Giddy with hunger, he grasps at their necks,
knee deep in icy water.

In the early dawn,
small imp,
Lazarus crouches beside an old man.
Seated on a tree branch
downwind of the hunt so they must squint to see.

The hunter hides in a hollow log with a leg of rancid deer,
drawing the bear deeper and deeper in.
Another man squats above, waiting at the knothole
to drive an arrow deep into the bear's head.

Sated, Lazarus rubs oil into his hair
shakes his limbs, huffing like a bear in the snow.
Pausing dizzy as he hears a hollow whicker.
The mare's time has come.

Creekside, groaning softly as her knees buckle.
White pills of lather
foam in the pockets of her flanks.
The foal slips neatly in an envelope of mucus
and the mare turns
to nip the cord and consume the waxy placenta.

A man aprons a ration of oats,
strokes the mare's neck in circular motions
and beckons to Lazarus.

Run your hands all over the colt. Trace every part of him.
Lazarus, he'll always be fond of your touch.

4.

At the waxing of the crow moon,
the most skilled midwife died coughing.

They are in open prairie,
no fluttering branches
or riparian caress.
So the girl whimpers in the corner of the tent
and turns her face into its dank scent.

Women pull her closer to the brazier.
Her shirt rucks up around her hips,
sharp lavender tributaries of veins
standing out across her thighs and belly.
This is her first, so she writhes when she should rest
and begs for her mother in fitful starts.

Fingers dipped in grease move nimbly between her legs.
She is cajoled

oiled slick,
cradled and lullabied.
In frustration, one woman slaps her hands together
and speaks sternly to her.

When she finally tears, the babies seem to hurtle out,
one on the other's heels.
She reclines on her elbows
as the women caress
their small mouths to her nipples.

The people sit around the fire.
Children are allowed to stay up
and meagerly gorge
on strips of dried venison, bear and swan.
in honor of the propitious birth of twins.
Mama, what is he saying?

Lazarus is lolling with his back

against his Mama's legs as the head man drones on.

> *He reminds us*
> *in the old times*
> *babble of the smallest children*
> *was most auspicious.*

A Mighty Pulverizing Machine

To each orphaned child—so long as you
remain close enough to walk to your
living kin you will dance, feast, feel
community in food. This cannot
stand. Eighty acres allotted.

To each head of household—so long
as you remember your tribal words
for village you will recollect that
the grasses still grow and the rivers
still flow. So long as you teach
your children these words they
will remember as well. This we
cannot allow.
One-hundred and sixty acres allotted.

To each elder unable to till or hunt—
so long as your old and injurious
habits sing out over the drum or flicker
near the fire you cripple our reward.
We seek to hasten your end.
Eighty acres allotted.

To each widowed wife—
so long as you can make your mark,
your land may be leased.
A blessing on your mark
when you sign it and walk closer
to your favored white sister.
Eighty acres allotted.

To each full blood—so long
as you have an open hand,
we shall fill it with a broken ploughshare.
One-hundred and sixty acres allotted.

To each half blood, each quarter strain—
so long as you yearn
for the broken ploughshare,
you will be provided a spade honed to razor
in its place. When every acre of your
allotment has been leased or sold,
you will turn it on yourself.
From that date begins our real
and permanent progress.

Winter Dance of the Oldest Child

1.

First light.
The oldest girl patches cracks in the wall
with sacking soaked
in potato starch.

Long strips of burlap
freeze solid
before she can work them
soft with the tips
of her fingers. Hint
of ice-shard light and smell
of last summer's harvest rot wafting
from the stacked cornstalks
insulating the cabin's western wall.

She papers the walls
with old newspapers from last year's missionary basket:
*American Agriculturist, Colman's Rural World, Prairie
    Farmer.*
Advertisements stare her down
all through winter's tallow light:
threshers, ploughshares,
leather martingales to tamp the necks of
draft horses into more pleasing lines.

On the table—pale green and amber beads
creep up unfinished moccasins
in a woven pattern of geometric corn shafts.

Her granny sleeps
under an unfinished morning-star quilt
still in piece work,
baste stitched.

2.

Drowsing on the milk stool,
the little brown Guernsey's soft eyes soothing
then piss-heavy tail
whipping her into reality.

Blunt cries of the baby
lowing through the cabin door
while her thumb and pointer finger
pinch into the warm milk,
dripping the heat down her throat in a shamed rush.

Her baby brother roots desperately at her
new breasts
through the calico warp of the apron—pain so bright and
        urgent
she thinks her body's been peeled from its skin.
She bites a whimper for their mother off
at the root of her tongue
as she trails a creamy snake of milk
down the channel of her pinkie finger
into the baby's mouth, crooning.

Whimpering and wide eyed, her brother
is like a green-broke colt, shying at the sound
of icicles splintering off the branches
and dimpling the ground outside.
Until, soothed by the milk,
his features wrap and tuck
into a mask of self-satisfaction
as he settles
into the straw.

And for the first time since waking,
the girl lets her body

settle for a moment too,
seeing milk, eggs, a finger of molasses, even some flour
on the table.

   3.

Winnowing afternoon light
plucks at the zigzag line
of spring-green seed beads
running up the seam of the leather moccasin.

The girl pauses momentarily
to cut the wick,
lick her needle,
dip her wet fingertip in the beads
and hold it studded in the light—
the beads like a cluster of pin headed beetles.

She's waiting for her father to ride home
with the start of the month rations.
Perhaps the preacher is
making the most of his captive audience
waiting out the back of the mission church.
The wicker baskets of salt pork
and coffee sitting in rows
just inside their line of sight.

But she worries
as the sky darkens
and she strains her ears against the quiet,
fatigued by the absence of hoof beats.
Her worry becomes a dancing
honey finger of whisky in her mind.

She flicks the beads from her finger
and huffs out to the coop
breaking an old hen's neck
with a breathless
snap over her shoulder.

Fries the bird, crackle of the skin on her tongue
the warmest thing she's felt in weeks.

Spring Thaw and the Land Runs

Zinc mining wives
traipse through the muck,
black leather toes
like picks. The station market in Neosho is a little reward
waved before them by prospecting husbands
to ease the burden of being a territorial spouse.
The exotic spread across the tines of the railroad tracks.

Women selling blankets
drape them across the hitching posts
for the settlers who come in waves.

A Shawnee girl places her beaded
moccasins on a bed of corn husks.
When she stands,
her baby brother
clings to her collar,
splays his bare toes
against her instep and shins
trying to crawl back up into her arms.
He dangles there unwilling
to put his feet back onto the ground.

The mining wives cluck
at the growing crowd of sooners,
offer the girl half price for a tiny set of moccasins,
not bothering to smile at the baby's antics.

The next season turns the prairie.

Ochre-threshing of the unassigned land runs:
Sac and Fox.
      Pottawatomie.
         Iowa.
            Shawnee.

No Longer

Removal—that sorrow trail
      but a weary exile just the same.

What tremor can be measured
in the pale wave of light
      that blazes a path of eviction?

Gazing at maps,
water calls attention through absence.
Lakes and river reaches
in Northeastern Oklahoma,
      the Scioto, Rio Grande, Kaw
            Columbia and Snoqualmie.

Watery seduction—
      migration's
            sultry stroke of fatigue.

To visualize the stones of a dry river bed—
      stubble of a razed corn field—
            cultivate the ankle's gaze.

To weather that expulsion path—
      hunch the shoulders into a perpetual wince.
Look back often.
Squint in the light
that shines on the backs of the knees.

Conceive a vista:
deliver hills sleek
      as a panther's shoulder blades.

Finger a rattlesnake fang
drag its miniature scimitar
through river clay

inscribe the clans
of a good genius
    society.

Measuring the Distance to Oklahoma

Shell shaking in the state
of the coin toss and sorrowful walk.

Weaving through the powwow grounds
grass stomped low and buzzing with flies
       your son walks two quick steps ahead of me
       to point out a tiny bow and arrow
       at a vendor's booth.

Rats scuttle in the grain silo.
The gentle clamor of the casino washes
through the parking lot.
A table is piled with half a dozen corn cakes,
each one embossed with the maker's thumbprint.
Your grandfather recounts
catching water moccasins as a boy
and spitting wads of tobacco down their throats
just to watch them squirm.

You sink onto a dusty quilt
gently pull the empty coke can from your boy's
sleeping fist
shake your head impatiently when your daughter whines for
       you to untie an intricately beaded belt from her regalia.
Child's arrow, capped with a pencil eraser
twirling in your fingers.

Ottawa County moon as seen from a distance:
pale vodka swirling in an open mouth.
Driving home on the frontage road,
green and riveted as a turtle's back.
Highway sketched into place by the broken black lines
of oil rigs at midnight.

Basement Storage at the Museum
of the American Indian

Down here humidity
serpentines and leaves pale crescents
on the sides of pots stacked at eye level.
Like saltwater crusting on a stack of shark fins.

After the thump and click of the doors locking behind us,
I resist the urge to panic.
The fluorescent light panels cast an amniotic blue
across the fingered ridges of the platters on the bottom
      shelves.

A comb has been dragged through these rows and held
    tight.
Can a connection be drawn to the children swapped at
    birth?

Someone whispers slowly that
it is a graveyard down here.

Visible discomfort spreads thorough the room
and a woman shakes her head
she wants to get home in time for the five o'clock news
which will profile a special
on children swapped at birth.

In the corner a pile of axes are stacked
relics from the first time
one was thrown over a shoulder
to mine for this museum.

The results were disastrous:
busted bentwood boxes and fractions of Anasazi polychrome.

Now those shattered pieces
have been strapped with sinew

or glued and re-glued in lines
like split lips and wet strands of hair.

A side cabinet is jerked out on oiled hinges
and beaded leggings sit, tagged with plastic
in static-resistant tissue paper.
The curator mumbles
distinctly Plains

and two people bicker about the Comanche influence
in northern New Mexico.

The tick of vents punctuate
cadences in the voice of the guard
who speaks with her back
to a shelf of Pojoaque red ware
and her arm draped across a coiled pot.

She pulls a chip of tile into her hands
blows the dust off
and returns it to its shelf.

Wars of Attrition

Mapping out territory
in 1984—
     my older cousin
         ditched me
in the scrub brush behind our granny's house

locked in a dog crate, five years old,
    howling.

Nine years ago, I taught her oldest child
how to write her name
on the back of a grocery list.

      My hand huge over her crayon
      clamped fist.

Paper plastered across her boxy little torso
like a peace treaty
as she galloped through the living room.

I was teaching seventh grade when my cousin died,
sugar gumming up her system
    like a glinting trail of dried snot.

Unable to focus,
    my mind
        flitted over the Cascades
        past a lake full of tree trunks
        poking up like rotten molars

landed in Eastern Washington
      next to my grandmother's backyard—
      next to my cousin's red curls.

A map is not a neutral document,
        one of my students parroted
        bubble eyed.

And I muttered
        that's right
            correct.

Vantage

Driving past Vantage:
    damp sign proclaiming ginkgo fossils
and iron sculpture of wild horses on the ridge.

At the turn of the last century,
Cayuse ponies were bred with European draft horses.
    A leaner, tougher work animal
        for the logging fields.

Trumpeter swans stitch
        the sallow slab of sky.
            Two birds swap point position
            to cut the air's polarity.

Path that pulls the taste
of mixed blood into my mouth.
Late February
and I am three weeks pregnant. I drive
        and the Columbia loosens
            my dad's easy silence.
He talks about his grandfather:
star musician of the Haskell Indian School Marching Band,
            telegraph operator, rodeo cowboy?
Tracking his family across
three states to hunt for big game
was habitual.

My grandfather,
dead within a week of my birth;
    I am told
        he looked at a Polaroid
        and proclaimed me an angry little Indian.

Late August in a post-depression labor camp
in the Mojave desert.

My dad was born; he might have been premature,
        covered with dark hair and sick
        enough to die?

Terraced sun shower wading through the cloudbank.
    Recollection becomes embrace?

At twenty-nine weeks,
the doctor's chart advises me—
        my child is two and a half pounds,
        like a Chinese cabbage.

Blinking heavy eyes and fluttering his newly formed lashes.
My hair still damp from swimming laps.
        Warning signs:
                severe headaches, excessive nausea, a
        change in reflexes.
Feel of the doctor's hand pushing me back onto the table.

In the hospital, I ask for books.
        Posters from old rodeos.
A photo of a Mimbres pot
from southern New Mexico
black and white line figures—
        a woman dusting corn pollen over a baby's head
        during a naming ceremony.
Medieval women
        ingested apples
                with the skins incised with hymns and verses
as a portent against death in childbirth.

Heparin Sodium
injected daily and nightly
        in a slow abdominal arc

incising my skin
        like a creation spiral; my hope apple.

Say splitting the rails of the body
to lay down a fence
between harm and one's young.

Terraced sun shower wading through the cloudbank.
My son at ten months
staring calmly at morning stars
during his naming.
The faint trail of corn pollen suspended
        in his fine, dark hair.

Ungelbah Davila

Outlaw Neon

This book explores the images of the American West. From the neon light of honky tonk barrooms to the Southwestern landscape to the railroad, dirt roads and grandmothers' living rooms.

UNGELBAH DAVILA

Country Music Gave Her the Courage to Break Your Heart

At the dance she was the peroxide blond in the Cody James
       hat,
a confederate flag on her buckle, a diamondback cowgirl
       coiled in a man's breast pocket.
A Camel menthol hanging out her mouth,
she danced like she was stomping out a wildfire,
proud, the way lilies are proud.
White calla of the neon light,
Valencia County's savior of wild salmon.
She kept reaching her foot ahead, even though you were
       leading.
That was before you fell in the parking lot and used her body
       like a crutch.
She carried you to a field, a Ruger 270 over her shoulder,
and shot beer cans in the headlights.
I used to skip the sad songs, she told you,
  but I don't mind them anymore.
In the morning the sun woke you up,
hungover in the bed of your truck.
Driving home past Isleta, you finally noticed the Buck Owens
       song
scribbled in the dashboard dust.

Passage

Girls all around
the world, in
Tokyo and New
York, catch
beauty rest on
fast trains, in
little black
dresses, the
color of winter
at six p.m.
when the day's
sweat has
moistened then
blistered the
skin on your
thighs, and
what do you do
'cause you're
not sleeping for
another eight
hours when
there's another
party and
another place to
be and another
five dollar drink
eating up your
rent and your
ticket out,
turning into
twenty then
twenty-five,
depending on
how little
you've had to

eat or how
much pain those
blisters are in,
and you know
better than to
expect any more
from that guy
down the bar
than from the
poems you have
scribbled on bar
napkins that
you keep in
your purse for
inspiration and
emergency
clean-up or as
toilet paper for
later when you
find yourself
pissing on the
side of the road
with that guy
from the bar
who's gunna
teach you the
important
lessons, like
how to order
whiskey, or
how to change a
tire, or how
never under any
circumstances
should you date

Geminis or
sleep with
neighbors or
redheads, no
matter how
drunk you are
even if he/she/it
agrees that
though the
lights are
unclear tonight
the concept of
them is more
vivid than usual
like the lights in
New York or
Tokyo or Spain,
but this isn't
New York,
Tokyo, or
Spain, tonight
it's just another
town with
another bar and
another man
and another
train going
south, north,
east, west to
nowhere.

The Distance of Breath

Her toes caress the sole of her boot,
keeping time to a sweet bottom note
like the lingering sound of a guitar
played at a kitchen table after work
by hands callused from holding wrenches, hammers,
pulling barbed wire between fence posts.
Hands that snag a woman's skin,
measure the space between bodies by the width of a thumb.
The distance breath travels before it cools.
She sips another man's beer,
leans back and stretches her leg out across the bar,
feels 60 miles into the night —
a length of smoky quartz, a snake stretched taught,
the color of sage brush moon shadows —
down La Bajada Hill to the bed where her lover sleeps
and dreams of something brushing against his chest.

Momma You Gotta Move

In a quick wedge of noon light you can see her tongue
    roll an "r" across the lip of her diet coke
when someone leaves to take out the trash.
You want to borrow it like a stick of gum,
hand it back when the flavor's gone,
    folded in a napkin under the table when her break is up.
Instead you go to the room behind the curtain
    with the chair the color of cherry Kool-Aid,
its arm rests balding beneath her knees,
and watch her teeth play peekaboo with her lips
    when she mouths the words *levee* and *break.*

Baby Dancer

That car took us clear through winter,
our ghosts rattling in the back like empty bottles,
   shivering against stone —
all the way to summer, where we ate warm peaches at
   Indian Springs,
where he pressed a red triangle on the dash —
where the radio is still playing that muddy Delta Blues.
It's Friday night now and the heat is smearing the seam
   of my stocking right off my thigh
onto his Cutty's ripped black seats.
Past the neons, home, his fingers slick on a bottle,
   wet to my touch.
Strip, he says, sudden and deep as a bass note, then,
   Goddamn baby.
My lace, like warm peaches, and the crickets hot, loud in
   the heat —
the label on the bottle calls it a velvet moon.
I tell him, *Play me the blues.*
I tell him, *I am ambassador of the love-sick woman*
   who pours whiskey on her heart like antiseptic.
I say, *Baby hand me that bottle, I don't need no glass.*
I tell him, *Light candles across the floor and turn the lights down,*
   we're having a seance in here.
There's a scarf over the lamp but I can see a little sweat on
   his lip.
He likes to watch me dance.
I like to watch him pull a cigarette from the pack with his
   lips.
In the flame I can see the dark outline of his nails
and I say, *Baby I'm arms-out here, waiting for the burning.*

2 AM, After a Moment of Uncertainty

Tonight,
with your tequilaed tongue and cold limbs,
that ran through midnight streets to be at my door,
I love you with the gentle yellow of first light
and the duende of red geraniums.
But also with the rainbowed backs of blowflies
the tender skin of white maggots,
because you too are the beauty of scorched earth,
broken porcelain, crushed apples.
And without you, I am the shivering dust
on a moth's wing before first snowfall.

The Leaves of Summer

The day Johnny Cash died, we sat hand in hand on the
   porch,
singing Folsom Prison Blues for the dog and the flock of
   blackbirds
that gathered in the apple trees to pay their respect —
the first leaves of summer falling, lazy, like the blossoms
that dusted the gravel lot behind the church that spring
where we practiced crushing cigarettes beneath the toes of
   our boots
like all our heroes, lighting matches just to watch them
   burn,
making wishes on their embers, because we felt too old for
   falling stars.

Last Dance

Dance me out of bed into the triangle of light
  the kitchen has snuck past the doorway
  onto the living room floor.
Dance me away from the faces that follow us.
Dance me out of my skin.
Dance me through the eternal winter,
  the frost bite on our lips.
Dance me through May, June, and July.
Dance me down the sidelines of war.
Dance me until my feet have forgotten my wounded side.
Dance with my bleeding hands and the ashes in my hair.
Dance with a halo of yellow finches perched
  against the storm in your head.
Dance me through prisons where woman hang from bars,
  where men remember the forgetting in the closed cells of
  their hearts.
Dance me until I have wept enough to heal water, dust and
  air.
Dance me when the stars fall and burn the flowered weeds
  at our feet.
Dance me in your arms the way a child holds a gun.
Dance me when I am bones and you are the feathers
  a raven leaves behind when it flies.

Ashiihí Asdsaani

I wonder at your jewelry,
at the way you comb your hair
and tie your belt around your waist,
how your voice is like water against river rocks,
flowing along the sides of your tongue.
I wonder at our reflections,
the gentle creases of your skin, soft as play dough
beneath my baby hands,
smoothed to look like mine.
I wonder as the light
catches the mother-of-pearl of your earrings,
white as salt crystals below Mount Taylor,
as abalone moons, a baby's face,
before it makes its first breath.

Iłnazbah, Shimásani the Spider

Together we card.
The wool, bathed and brought in from the sun,
oily between flat brushes, dry,
scraping, a gentle ripping sound through their metal teeth,
our hands thick with lanolin,
making small piles of sticks as we clean.
Everything smells of sheep in the sunshine.

Her spool turns right, right, right
like the rotation of the world,
spinning yarn, coiling around her feet,
we talk about that crazy bilagáana Jay Leno
and the pictures in *National Geographic*.

The vinyl has thinned and split
where shimásani sits counting
the design of her weave,
a breathy two-languaged rhythm,
soft and grey as steam
drifting from a kettle on the wood stove.
On the couch, I lull to geometric sounds —
her comb softly striking one, two, three, pause,
tapping down the yarn,
strumming the weft,
t'aał'aai, naaki, taa'.

Lamination

Awakened by the drizzle of October rain
that causes waxy yellow leaves
to cling to glass like soggy cereal,
I cannot separate it from the sound
of the fountain in the courtyard.

I pretend a tangling of toes,
knees stacked one on top of the other,
lying laminated to your side by sticky skin
and a thick layering of quilts piled against the morning.

You are not here, but I sleep naked anyway,
enfolded in my own limbs,
shivering like the last petals of summer impatiens,
lying on your side of the bed for warmth,
I sooth myself to sleep with sounds like lamination.

Odessa

I taste your name, sliding along my tongue
and teeth like an unfurling copperhead.
At sunset a rig drills beyond your rosy neon lights,
panhandle black against an orange Texas sky, setting
and rising a slow, oily waltz.
Your men drift in off the field, Odessa,
their blue norther bodies
humming honky tonk hymns, nails
workingman dark in the dashboard glow of an FM station.
Suck the smoke from their mouths, Odessa,
and blow it hard and slow so it rises
far above the barroom haze, settling in a halo
around a sticky jukebox, playing
three generations of Hank against a dirty wall
where I first felt you arch your aching back against me,
your whiskey breath sweet as rotten fruit.

Sumbios

We found a kitten in Oklahoma.
I carried her inside my jacket,
her belly gray and spotted,
curled against my stomach, my arms
hugging your waist, our legs
molded around your motorcycle,
our bodies moving in unison against the wind,
the semis, the black top rushing beneath us
across Texas.
At a neon in Lubbock our arms crisscrossed,
searching for a piece of the other,
the kitten sewn between us, humming
a tiny one cylinder
and in the distance a storm, singing
sweet as a steel guitar
across the oilfields outside of town.

'54

I keep you in the back of my throat like words I used to
    know,
or like the scent of chemical solvent and cigarette smoke,
when I helped you rebuild the engine,
cleaning bolts in the sink in brown liquid like lung water.
I held my breath then, turning my head towards the door.
Now I breathe into my hands to refresh my memory,
inhaling air trapped in warm palms, blowing on glass,
cutting the shape of your face into the frost,
erasing it with my breath like I did
when my fingers doodled stick figures of a girl and boy
on the passenger window you installed so I would stay
    warm
that April, riding next to you in a snow storm,
driving through Flagstaff to Vegas with no heater or
    wipers.
Baby, my love for you is a lopsided cart, broken down
    Ford,
this old '54 that got us there and back,
but I'm still lost on the side of the road, thumb out, hoping,
trying to glue my wheels back together,
digging in the dirt for every piece I've lost,
blowing on my hands for warmth.

Viva 13

It all melted away in a hotel room in Vegas,
your body inside me, on the balcony, the floor, behind open
    blinds,
hoping someone would see, cause we could've been
    anybody.
Under the MGM Grand's emerald green shadow,
we imagined what the strip would look like after the
    apocalypse —
a million gaping sockets where light bulbs used to be.

It's a spring night, and if it were 1950, I'd be Bettie Leah.
We cry wasabi tears at The Orleans
eating sushi and Singapore street noodles.
Elvis, black and white and grainy,
knees wobbling on at least fifty screens, playing swing at
    any hour,
round Americans and slick black Japanese.

We spit on the Bellagio, puked in the parking lot, rolled
    dice
drunk on whiskey, rum, whatever and won two hundred
    dollars.
Spent it at Frankie's, sunburned and smashed on blue syrup
Green Gasser tiki drinks, the orchids in women's hair,
plastic combs, cuffed Levis and rolled up sleeves,
Cock Grease, Layrite, Morgans, and Sweet Georgia Brown
    boys
leaning against Buicks, Cadillacs, Chevys and Fords,
glowing beneath neon dollar signs.

The Birth of O

Sucking your dribble,
a gentle translucence,
glistening against the U of a lip,
lax like a section of blood fruit,
split on the counter — orange,
an olive,
swirling past the lip of your glass,
past the swish of your tongue,
past my fingers against your neck,
into the pit of your gut, down
chased by a clear martini trickle,
sliding between your breasts,
to your sweet, indelible Y,
that I rise to meet in a perfect, oblong O.

Black

Motor oil on my knees
and under my nails
and on my bare feet
like the air outside,
like his shirt,
like his hair
and the outline of his tattoos.
Like the punching bag
that I right hook,
left jab,
kick,
like my skirt that wraps,
like whiskey labels,
like cigarette ashes,
bruises,
smeared makeup
my fists.
And then I'm down on all fours
or up on all twos
or down on both knees,
my high heels
my lace panties
lost under someone's four-door Sedan,
and I am
oil,
night skies,
garage dirt,
the insides of bodies,
an unspoken question.

Dirty Halo

Woodsmoke will always remind me of the tattoos
   on your knuckles
as you shifted into reverse that night in November
when we went to Gallup and you left me in the cold,
   too bitter to snow.
That night I spent shivering in a Greyhound station,
waiting for the first bus to Albuquerque to roll in,
   just before sunrise,
and the Navajo boy in the flannel shirt
who slept in the seat beside me the whole way back
while I watched the sun come up over I-40,
casting the desert childlike in the sudden dawn.
And that morning that I burnt your picture in the bathtub,
its ashes floating around my body like a dirty, gray halo
   while the water grew cold,
my skin shrinking against my bones, your black flecks
speckled against my limbs when I walked to the kitchen
   to pour a glass of Chardonnay, and cry,
my wet footprints in the hallway, evaporating slowly with
   the day.

In The Time of Tulips Bent Beneath Her Feet

She spent the summer after high school
climbing through his window, its frame
dividing her into a pair of legs, outstretched
like skinny wings, one hooking
through like the letter L, the other
pushing out of the flowerbed, its foot
a naked arch amongst the tulips, whose stems
grew sideways beneath her feet.

She was 17, her hair blowing
across a barber shop floor,
from a plastic bag, her fingers, across the backyard,
a flock of thin sparrows in the breeze,
one lock for every prayer, for every line,
for every drug inside his vein
until there was nothing left to cut.

Looking for Monkeys by the Rio Grande

Holding hands on a pier
where a river used to be,
we marvel how the moonlight
reflects on the sand,
a color that hasn't been named yet.
We decide on silver.
After we leave,
I slip a poem in your pocket.
It's written like a balloon
twisted into the shape of an animal.
I think it's a tiger,
but you call it a dog.
The cottonwoods release white tufts
that stick to your hair.
I imagine that you are the boy in the tree house
that I loved when I was eight.
At the end of your street,
where it dead-ends at the zoo,
we look for animals through the fence,
and are instead astonished
to see birds fly from my fists.

The Year of Eclipses

Lying in an apartment in the valley
we were a broken horizon,
our backs and bellies pushing down the ground,
holding up the sky, pushing back the water.
Everything was threatening to rearrange itself.
Oceans rising from their beds like frustrated lovers,
taking the earth by force,
her body cracking like salty winter sidewalks.
It was the year of eclipses,
and the sun and moon played vanishing games in the sky
while we knelt on the earth, crying.
Spring came and it snowed without ending.
I fought blizzards most weekends,
arriving at your door like a salmon, bleeding,
floating home again come Monday.
I told you how the fish were dying, the birds, the bees,
how the animals were leaving.
In the morning we listened to the monkeys
scream from their cages at the zoo,
and at night I felt stars coming through the roof
without your back to shield me,
while the monkeys, they never stopped screaming.

The Valley

I walk down Coal to 13th,
from the store
where groceries are painted on the wall,
labeled in black —
leche, cigarrillos, jabón, carne,
toilet paper, coconut hand soap,
a notebook and Saint Lazarus candle in my bag —
recipes for the poor.
Sun on my hair,
in my tattoo,
burning the colors of the *barrio* —
the woman who sits under a red umbrella
on purple wisteria rooftop,
the neighbor's blue hydrangeas
lined up against the wall in black pots,
the low cars,
gold, teal, primer gray,
barking South Valley dogs,
and men gathered around an ice cream cart,
bullshitting in Spanish,
turtle doves that croon
mid-day *la llorona* songs,
guitar music in houses dark from rain clouds,
sticky from afternoon bodies,
my lover's skin
salty from working hard today,
his sweat burning sweet booze,
gleaning a breeze off the river,
drinkin' lonely.
I thumb a necklace of keys to get inside his door.

The Citrus Vendor

who sells fruit from the tailgate of his Ford,
wrapped in flannel and denim beneath a shy December sky,
has faded letters on his knuckles that move like typewriter
   keys
as he quarters a grapefruit with his knife and watches the cars
      go by.

Tea Cup

Whose chipped lip his whiskers tickle,
sits lonely on the shelf or dirty in the sink,
day dreaming about warming his hands
and the intimate design of his greasy fingerprints.

She wonders what if feels like to be Cigarette,
who informs his breath and visits the cavern of his lungs.
How romantic to be ashes in the bottom of a broken cup.

Tea Cup has been waiting for him to come home
and touch her with his soapy hands again.
It's crowded on the counter and she is feeling jealous
of Fork and Spoon and the way he looks at Plate.

She wishes he would take her like Sugar in his coffee
and taste her on his lips before she disappears completely.

1-800-GET

Woman, how you walk, how you bend, how you stretch
    back like the bygone
goddess of a sweet sixteen Coney Island roller coaster date
who left me riding the Ferris wheel when I couldn't stand
    for what felt like a century,
when I tasted cherry chap-stick every time I ate for a week,
    hearing K-pop songs like *Gee,*
tormenting me into poet-hood, tossing me amongst the
    Chucks, the Bobs, Elliot and e.e.,
imagining the similarity between your eyes, your nipples,
    your bush and my mother's morning tea.
Woman, oh how I long to stand outside the door and think
    of Buddhist fountains when you pee.
Oh how I long to initiate a food fight in a B&B in Provence
    and eat blue cheese off you.
How I long to read the elegy of your hair, those strands that
    shhh like a pair of mating S's
and wallow between the tops of your tall sock without a
    care, without a where, without a why.

Primitive Technologist

I have an Internet stalker named Steve.
Steve has dreadlocks and grows monstrous leeks,
(I'm talking like 5ft long
because his aim is length first, then girth—
for practical reasons you understand)
and surfs the net for CUTE (in caps) young girls
to share with his rock star of a wife,
the illustrious Tweeter.

Steve gets upset when I call him a hippie,
(though he clearly is)
because in the dial-up mountains
of Bumblefuck, California,
"hippie" is a derogatory household term,
and Steve is a man, you understand,
    not a stereotype.
Instead, Steve likes to think of himself
as a primitive technologist,
the poly-amorous, leek growing kind.

Steve is my biggest fan.
I make him believe in God.
I make him hungry for cupcakes.
He advises me not to let my icing melt,
    to stay spunky,
and to do a better job at leading him on
lest he lose interest
and find another CUTE young thing to stalk.

Steve is now a part of my personal network.

Steve sees substance under my
EXTREMELY CUTE exterior
and hopes that I'm not an
enormously obese

mole covered,
crew-cutted,
pimply,
white male
alternately eating pork rinds,
scratching his ass
and masturbating with the same hand
while the other hand is permanently
formed over a computer mouse.

I assure him I am.

Steve likes me 'cause I'm CUTE
and quirky.
He hopes he's made that clear.

Today Steve made me his desktop picture
because that's what any good stalker would do.
He's committed to the task.
I'm thinking of demanding a candle-lit altar
and some dead animals.
Maybe a leek or two.

Smiling Shoulders at the Flying Star Cafe

Struggling with the thick glass door at 8th and Silver
you hear a girl's voice behind you say,
"Shit's heavy huh?"
Thick, sweet and familiar, a from-the-cradle voice.
Like warm caramel on a sundae.
Like summer sweat and sunflowers.
Like sticky bud and cut offs, mud and a white tank top.
Like older cousins. Like Woodstock '94
and the girl in the picture off the album jacket
who you worshipped
because she was 16 and you were 8 and she had boobs
and blonde hair and a beautiful slouch, her shoulders
curving into the shelf of her clavicle
making a half moon of her body.
A grunge baby-doll-type goddess sitting stoned
with flowers in her hair
and you were some shy kid on a ranch,
and everyone in the world was watching MTV but you.
When you turned around she was grown,
frail and bold in big sunglasses,
coke skinny and smoky ordering a bag of sweets.
You admired her anyway,
the syrupy slur of her words
and the weight of her wonderful slouch, her shoulders
still bending into herself like a hug,
like the mouth of a smiley face.

Sex in the Soda Shop

The boys all want to be Elvis, the girls Marilyn, but
their parents don't let them put peroxide in their hair, so
they bop around like little Norma Jeans,
all bubblegum and ponytails.
They smell like frosting, like
sunscreen, sweet tarts, cigarettes purloined
from mother's purse.

I wanna rock for them, roll for them, glow pink and
blue for them. I wanna play 'em something that gets rough
slowly, something mean and a little dirty. I
wanna show 'em to a room in the Heartbreak Hotel, tuck
    'em
in, croon 'em a bedtime song.

And the boys, well if they're cats
they like to mix a little shoe polish in their Morgan's before
they slick their hair, cuff their Levis, cock
a leg against the wall when
they lean, skinny,
freckle faced babes,
duck tales pitch black and greased back. They
strut like cocks,
sorting out their manhood, carving
their niches out of blood and asphalt
in the parking lot, on the field, in the backseat of
their father's borrowed Chevrolet —
picking out something to carry them
through the next sixty years, through
paradise suburban tract houses, through
wives and babies, through
beer and whiskey, through
divorce, remarriage, and death,
slow or quick, nine-to-five
turned endless days.

But now it's all white and black and white
again, it's hot and loud, a driving bass line, it's
girls, oh yes, it's girls,
sliding nickels down my slot.
It's shake, spin, play it again,
it's a boney hip against my side,
it's leather, pomade, cut grass and gasoline, screaming
Teenage Heaven, hands,
thighs and sticky mouths, lipstick and sweet
   perfume.
It's the sway in your pelvis, the twist, the swing.

Two Cigarettes

Matt wants tequila
because he's lost his wife
lost his kids
his job
his dog,
his mind.
He reminds me of neglect,
of fathers,
and lovers,
and husbands
who'd rather give you a song
than diamonds or gold.
He's a regular honky tonk merry go round.
The sight of him alone
makes me weep in my beer.
These are the qualities I look for in a man.
They should sound like a Patsy Cline song
when they yell
and laugh
the broken laugh
of a broken man,
that smells like the beer
he had for breakfast,
or dinner the night before.
The next of kin to the wayward wind.
The kind of laugh that flirts
with madness,
and big, blonde, buxom bar flies,
nicotine scourged and randy,
swaying in darkness.
The kind of laugh that sounds
like heavy dinner plates
being thrown against stucco.
The sound of it gives me goose bumps,
alerts my senses

for the cold water plunge
of a rescue mission.
Endless submersion.
Two cigarettes in an ash tray.

The Boys of Burque

Cockgrease, Layrite, Morgans and Sweet Georgia Brown
boys, in broken down Fords,
in drive-through lines, and dirt lots
genuflecting beneath winged Cadillacs and Biscaynes,
nuclear green, Communist red, rattle-can black, back down,
top up, East past Rio Grande,
past motel row, past neon, past go,
toward broken bottled burro alleyways,
toward ephemeral dawns crashing through windshields
drunk on whiskey, Pabst, tequila sunrises,
singing Hank, singing Cline, singing
that blackbird lullaby, that love me tender
moment of a setting moon.

1,000 Miles
for Daddy and Dwight Yoakam

You hummed me to sleep with
every great cowboy ballad ever written,
those crushing midnight trains,
those dark horses, galloping through
every cloud of dust I've ever made
turning my pickup around, down
every lonesome goddamn dirt road,
I've ever traveled at dusk.
Through every shot of whiskey
in every bar in every goddamn town
where I ever got thrown out
and had to walk home barefoot
and sleep it off alone.
Through every man and every hat
in every motel lobby along I-40
I ever went up the stairs with
because he looked like you.
Through every cool pearl button
on every white shirt my eye make-up
ever bled against during every sad song
at every rodeo dance
I've ever gone to since I was twelve.
Through every moment that I could bend
one more finger on my right hand
for every time you've ever said *I love you*.
Through every bad spill
I ever got up and walked away from
and through every cast of every bone
I ever broke that wasn't too close to my heart.

KRISTI LEORA

Dark Swimming

A narrative through wrenching spaces in the life of one descendant wrestling with post apocalyptic identity, grounded by persistently supportive ancestors and helpers determined to see their blood survive and resist colonial assimilation through disembodiment.

Thanks to my family, my ancestors, the Niagara region and all of its foliage, waters, and animals, the winds of the four directions, Juliana Spahr, the people I have lived with and loved, the Puget Sound region and all of its ascendants and descendants, and the future.

We are an embodiment of the divine that has spurred us into existence. The word *I* deliberately does not appear within these pages.

KRISTI LEORA

I.   *backdrops: before birth*

One Landscape's Possible Story
Niagara Gorge circa the Silurian era
beyond time and into memory
look back:
dolomite floor
saltwater sea
tropical   exotic
tread careful
this was not open space
                    at   one   time
            humans cannot exist submerged
                    now a gaping crack stands
            in the earth's surface
            once the same area would flood and drain
            like moods
            reminders of Silurian life
            once a home for dolphins
            delicate coral reefs
            tiny traveling seahorses

Niagara's Whirlpool Rapids In Preparation for Human Life
meteorites strike
a sheet of ice
the now Great Lakes
heat: flaming stars grind into planet
burn an arc into the globe, a birth
fresh water for millions of years
that plan still works as designed
despite abuses
coiled pools of water
suck stray fragments below— look close

for silhouettes of dolphins
within the water's mist
recalling cleaner days
before the water was harnessed
before machinery and engineering
said: we need devices to distribute power
when really
power can be drawn from the water
and into the mind into the heart
with no other tools
and once a man
Anishinaabe
walked the earth and did just that
            following a great silence
            while the Creator of the universe
            thought of ways to execute the vision
            that would connect the human mind
            and the human heart
            to all living things in the periphery

Shore of Lake Ontario, Today
            Once this area was silent
            now temper and weight hang
            in the air in the water
            stuttered grudges accusations
            scattered activists mourn the tragedy of choice
            (it comes with being human)
here the beach stands survivor
the aftermath of progress
progress its possibilities
rife with ways to go wrong
to misinterpret
all that is heard
now: all we know is noise
and temperature, hot or cold

a few humans sit in cars
on the bluff above the beach
resistant to walk down and touch it
threatened by the flying rat
the seagull the timeless
        routine of seabirds
        rising and falling above the water
        windshields deny their vitality and grace
        the birds confuse plastics for food
        and choke on the death of throwaways
        gone is the equilibrium of coral reefs
        effortless they sustained all life
                a truth: without humans life thrived
                and thrives
changing its face sometimes
                        often
        balance and survival are what sustains life
human control   extends inward only

Echoes of the Timeless in All
Seeing the tendencies of humans
the voice of perhaps an extinct clownfish
certainly a fool some say, speaks:
"life as a seagull would be better"
and in a stray mind a voice echoes
gulls eh
as humans rummage
through a garden center
standing in proximity to the bodies
of these connected waters
gulls yap silly sounds
above tension and drama
dead-set on snatching some herring
in an ideal habitat
French fries will do just fine here

the bird just needs something tangible
to sustain itself
doesn't hunger for dominion
so maybe the simplicity
the grace is superior in risen flocks
but eventual tragedy bubbles
even skyward
and the gull
the individual gull is smashed
its body falls flat
returning to the darkness
that occurs just before creation
returns to the great silence
we each greet
alone

Dark Swimming

As spirits we made the decision
we were offered the gift
to become formed beings
extensions of another's vision
we agreed to lower to the human realm

Going under we knew the risks
shaky at first but so alluring
was the depth
the idea the submersion
as humans
we come to and from the water
to walk above the ground
to become creatures that speak
not separate from the current
though its forms and ours oppose

Now we know
just because a body leaves
one sect of the universe for another
the soul brings its work, agreed upon
there is no escape
just as there is no measure of time
wind remembers this rumble this vibration
pushes that back into the face
one mirror of creation
one reflected storm
the madness in each and every
comes out sometimes a rumbling
quivering mouths tremble to speak
disturbances give voice to each one
through the vessel words emerge
sometimes soft like whale spray
sometimes aggressive like Mount Saint Helens
sometimes it's like dolphins

arcing over a sunny saltwater surface
sometimes it's like New Orleans flooding
under the brashness that, also, is us

Nothing can come between our bodies
and the deep of the water
our essence matches and yet
we are different and we
do not entirely dissolve
on the way down
unsure what lay beneath
unsure if we will make it back
lost even
waves threaten our airway
the passage where breath
first came through from creation
breath: our tether to everything that is

Wind's force is strong
beyond the limits of human speech
language is after all
brief and fleeting
so what do we have then
our galaxy our mistakes
grief sways like the airy leaves
on a sighing willow tree
before our arrival there was knowing
in some depths we'd forget
how to swim
we'd forget origin
the feeling sometimes would be
wildness from the deep
trying to pull us under
and we said yes anyway
to join the realm of formed beings

the birthed the living
sent forth
with blessings of the Mystery

Known or not
all is held together
as it has been and will be held
by layers
the world's invisible veins
in this together
we are in this together
among uncertain elements
inside unsteady bodies
we arrive and return
predisposed to keep our heads
above and aware though
at any moment no mistakes
like the sun
all will vanish

II. *living and integration: the time of the seventh fire*

Perimeters: Their Revolution

In the cold thickness of night a now departed relative crossed the Saint Lawrence alone in a canoe carrying our sacred wampum belts. She wanted to ensure with the move of the family the belts were safe and not forgotten. One belt spoke of the Seven Fires prophecy; it spoke of a time when the Original Peoples' fragmented families would return to their beginning ways of life following an influx of hardship and destruction. Another, the Jay Treaty belt, spoke of a vast and borderless continent, free passage for all Indigenous people within, despite the imposed borders of invaders. Royal Canadian Mounted Police would later chase after the belts, subversive against the closed door of our ancestors' house after the family had been pushed into stiff pews of Catholicism and conformity. Police wanted to capture and destroy physical evidence proving Anishinaabe vision: proving that belief was heard understood and agreed upon by both parties.

Though the barrier of language persists, stubborn like the delicate and enduring shell of the belts, the teachings survive laws and wars—brothers and sisters, ancient truths will not be disregarded. Ours is not a system that supports separation of organic matter; as relatives we are to respect facts of the universe, respect extensions of matter beyond our superficial selves. We have sameness with water earth, quahog shells— even scientists are catching up now, informing a dubious public that water is made from stardust: it's stars that sustain us, water has feelings, stars have feelings, knowingly or not, we balance one another.

Years ago men stood at the base of water's extended canyons drawing absurd maps of ownership, lines that have come to stand for the differences between skin and tongue. Still, there are ways to know better. In this time of the seventh fire many cousins and aunties remember a grandpa's words even after oppressive facades of government and church demanded this family choose the way of their civilization. He'd say, hushed: that is not our way. We have our own way. He was long gone when this descendant's time on earth began but he sees us returning one by one to the sacred fire, the sacred path, where the belts originated. Despite the relentless assault of an outer world that demands ownership through any means necessary, assimilation and genocide have failed here. The belts, their teachings are remembered.

Much time has passed since that cold, thick night, the night our belts moved over a liquid path composed of the element known to this descendant as an ill relative, in this day and age. Descendant's body thumbs a nose at the large structure that tries to distinguish what is called the U.S. from what is called Canada. Its mirrored windows make bare, ravenous clones of eyeballs, the skittish cameras scour traffic. The border creates a divide in the water below its bridges: the stream is lined with toilet waste, the water is streaked with leaden stains— so polluted is this water that it has become physically heavier than other waters. Weary with the burden and grief of one that tries to persevere through impurity. Dumped metal is sunk well below the surface. Trash and confusion litter the horizon.

Border patrol stands by waiting to be useful, waiting for human drama to catch fire with primal urges when they rise to the tangible surface. Sometimes it feels appropriate to stop and strike up a conversation with one of the guards, to share ideas, maybe present some they haven't heard before: greed and insolence—never delivered gently. The breath of life— always delivered gently. No one really "owns" anything so the whole set up, including his or her job, is kind of a guffaw, a joke. But snug semi-hysterical gun holsters tight around the waist remind: it's doubtful we'd laugh together if they were presented with these things. Past interactions recall incidents when they've insisted with hyper vigilant inspection of tribal ID cards: some day they say, the time will come when we have to make a choice of citizenship. The time will come when tribal cards, the ones they created for us to identify ourselves to them, would not be enough. With such a temper and mouth it seems right, in a moment like that, to keep walking, save the conversation for another time. Blood of this descendant is often satisfied to know its memories and truths, that borders, like these guards and their sense of self importance, are illusions.

Night comes for the extended family of our beautiful ancestors. The moon rises above and humanly in composition there is nothing different from those guards and this descendant. Still, there are souls who deny what has happened, those who ignore the face of the moon on water, where there is clear connection and timeless renewal, gifting. The only separation between groups of humans is the tongues they speak with, despite a contrived world of owned and divided places. With imaginary lines with all that division no one, nothing, is in balance. Despite these impositions we remember the importance of understanding each other, from the floor of waters upward. This on the face of an earth that has, for some, become a valueless collection of partitions driving dissent into its core, driving humans further from each other.

Ascension

Some relatives appear
to help one another
and in some moments
the massive world seems small, soft, built
like the body
around a blazing core

To run at one time
seemed impossible
rubbery legs rickety body
layers of doubt and disbelief
how could this body move
with smashed discs
excessive fat
weakened muscles
one wondered

and similarly
how could one look at
the continent's largest
self-renewing freshwater source
see it ever overcome
the hacking and rerouting
of engineering structures
the assault of discarded
steam engines nuclear waste
disintegrating under the
surface/ poison grinding
into rocks beneath
decayed remnants slithering
onto disparate shores
three-eyed fish appearing
the illness of the relative
lent itself: it is not, said the water
only humans

who have been enslaved
by the colonial process

One dark afternoon
a human being
aided by an approaching relative
the thunder
runs alongside the water
fueled by a brutal despair
we know that our species
has brought illness
and the effect is illness for all

Body moves against strong currents
on the right
rational side of the body
a west wind pushes the left side
where the heart lives
toward water's whirlpools—
shoulders hunch, spine arcs
      like subtle curve of earth
limbs hang, bone marrow daunts
      as of weighted asphalt
body wants to crumble/unrest
splits the body in two halves
      one half trusts the power
of the water's spirit to renew itself   renew faith
to inspire better choices in humans
      the other half
is tired and wants to harm itself: despondent
expects
the worst
is used to the worst
almost wants the worst
so it will all be logical

But the relative the water
makes its vibration louder sound arises from the water
        heartbeat   beneath the water   intensifies
spine stops sagging
        body pulls itself together
        ancient rhythms gain strength
    patterns of wave and current form lines
like a collection of perfect vertebrae

Trust is only the beginning
            the body must stay upright   spine straight
head up   if you want to be heard
with help from spirits
in the water   in the air   in the creation
a running body flies forward
there is a return
a trot a skip it snowballs
an avalanche of force
this body is gifted power
as if hollow weightless
            both halves united
            faith reborn
                    again

Notes From Cellular Memory

Walking from the library
away from insulated windows
snow dances
welcoming winter's arrival
stunned flakes wander
bury a path over blood
spilled on the sidewalk
evidence
the world sometimes
lowers to brutality
          body senses pain
blood remembers
a whir of activity   ancestors
their faces their fires
their lives woven
into the elements
blood remembers surviving
winter without insulation
no buildings no heaters
making it through
was the question

Regenerated cells
successive organs
skeletons and marrow
know what it is
to live outside the tribe
to arrive at a point in history
when humanity is forced
to learn: we are the same
          a species

It's a different kind
of endurance now
blood quantified by institutions

contained within a body
a miracle it's still here
warmth circulates
as the walk home begins
the library becomes a speck
in the horizon
descendant's body moves
like dancing against snow
against cold/against dark
matter and nothingness
in white space
between snowflakes/back
in the library
are collected photos of ancestors
complete with body counts
before tolerance
was such a marketable virtue
on this continent

Photos tell stories
our tribes our people labeled
by which massacre they perished in
by what Anglicized word
describes who they were
never referred to
as we have known ourselves
since the beginning of time
Anishinaabeg the original people
Ongwehonwe: the genuine people
photos record deaths
names exact identities absent
yet
academically defined history
does not matter
in the living body

eyes remember their smiles
hair remembers warmth
ears feel laughter
heart feels sorrow
blood remembers when
all we knew of ourselves
was that we were a part
of the creation
the earth   the air
the fire   the water

It was the seventh generation forward
our faces they saw
in dreams they prayed
to have descendants
when they wept
for the loss of our ways
when the attack
on our humanity arrived
with manifest destiny
it was our hearts
they were reaching for
as brothers of the U.S. Army
dug wider and deeper graves
our ancestors
our blood remembered the possibility of us
in their hopes that
we shall live
at least one surviving body
on this brutish winter afternoon
knows all of our human insides
match the strata of the earth
stepping over blood
where previous generations perished
to make way

for sidewalks and institutions
faithful
in a future of survivors who remember
where they came from

They Snap When Broken

January brings a bitter surface
it hardens us dries us
skin so cold so raw it's numb
bark smears with salt and grit

Even so
earth's bodies vibrate;
a belligerent heat inside
wants to break free
to be light/hence the burn
to uncoil
the drive to fall away

In a silent forest shocked to stillness
a slick sheen of frozen matter
covers all
for weeks now
no tears just ice
among a gallery of trees
one cold body breaks down
the trees stand steady
wear the same colors
as skin as hair
ruddy depths of heart
shades of shattered maroon
taffeta crimson
willows, oaks, maples, dogwoods
sprouting upward
shooting deeper

Like brothers silent in their acceptance
they know this is where
their human sister comes to cry
grief streams from eye sockets
that wish to see clear

to see through crystal

The sadness falls and is accepted
the earth accepts us as we are
as it is/ an immobile frozen walkway
receives saltwater drops
while flecks of ice break away
to shatter from distant branches

As the globe pulsates
the compositions change
energy redistributes
in an impartial atmosphere
a face is warmed
a body tingles
reawakened
hearts inside
the fires inside each being
drive away an unnamed sadness
that once rendered us
unable to move,
unable to change.

Setting Fire

1) FOR CERTAIN PLANT SPECIES

because of you, greasy knuckles, swollen
demands, instructive mouth, when autumn came
the sound of rustling leaves was disgusting and so
were sweet earthy smells of space
covered in dead foliage
stripped of chlorophyll
merely changing with time

2) THERE IS ONLY ONE WAY TO SURVIVAL:

littering the ground, a constant reminder of
the woods, the remote quiet in the deep of them
where as a child, back there it became clear:
you can hear every animal movement

3) Through The Blaze Of A Wildfire

as they scurry to find food, companionship, or
whatever it is animals do way behind the houses
where you taught just what you liked
it is unnecessary to humiliate you
with the details here, certain you remember:
to hurt you now is not the point
despite what is said of revenge

4) THE INTENSITY OF THE HEAT

arriving at acceptance: our souls so reluctantly are
tethered entangled and though it seems
you stole unreturnable things

to go onward
to forgive to understand is now the work:
revisiting the dark woods
that were not quiet when you took
what you wanted back there—

5) The Only Way, The Only Hope For Some

that space at one time was a home
even amid the disgust/misguided energy
how else to get through that, but
think: bless this indignity
praise this shame
without it
returning to the palm of the Creator
to rest in an uneven coil
this body would not know the relief
of a still tongue, unfettered hands

6) Some Tightly Wound Seeds

returning, there is no trace of the taking
and perhaps your face has changed
through these years, no longer starved
benign contentment wafts through the air
memories shed like fallen deciduous leaves
crisp in autumn air

7) Need The Heat To Burst Forth

set everything on fire said the hands
in our woods

but only burned
a tiny smoldering mass of our history
the smoke cleared a way for new memories
fanning a smudge
in the little deaths of autumn
in this ritual brought forth
smoke pours through
and the traumas extinguish—

Aboriginal Remains

The story you told
was of a people destroyed
we agreed on one thing at least
nothing would ever be the same
as it once was
pointless to try
you continued: only the ugly
and boring animals are left
we are how they call us in the books—
a colonized people
the old ways died
our spirits our future went
with our massacred ancestors

In your story then
you say we are left to wither now
powerless, smothered
by what some called their destiny
our still-beating hearts were buried
in the dust of dirt paths
before we even descended to earth   yet
even now parts of the land remain
untamed: untapped
you've been released
a graduate of rehab
still you see nothing redeeming here
even enveloped by wildness
even when you recognize

the language of the raccoon

    whose face reminds us of the masks
    we might not even intend to wear
    whose dexterous paws defy human machinery
    whose habit is to wash and honor food before eating

the language of the deer

    who teach us to look
    at each other in innocence
    soft eyes with a thin skull
    of two sides: reason or intuition
    both ears for listening

the language of the lizard

    with a belly soft and oblong
    stays close to the vibration of earth
    detaches a tail when it senses
    it's about to become prey
    adaptability of full senses

the language of the dragonfly

    who maintain power over land and water
    translucent wings somehow mirror light
    certain of when two wings are enough
    and when to use all four

Your first day home
a monarch butterfly parks in front of us
the rehab labeled you ready to re
enter society and yourself
as if it was their decision
the monarch says
you will stay there
as long as you remember
how to fly and that
dearest relative
they have not seen or had
the best of us
yet.

And Here They Said Apocalypse

The great cleansing
has come. We watch
sheets of earth crumble away
as it was said they would
contemporaries witness
abuse's aftermath
the LCD screen glows with
deafening animation
like a sporting event

Darkness arrives
unsatisfied spirits
people who walked on
after absorbing chemical warfare
assorted cancers
"well who cares
about Greenland, anyway?"
asks the nearby woman
who'd rather know
a different kind of score

The wisdom of departed relatives
how to care for the earth
to respect the feelings of the waters
seems to have died
better days memories packed in a soft belly
among layers of bone and dirt
but the truth is
that we are each born
with that knowledge
and despite the work of those
who would dispirit the landscape
and feed the coming generations
with paint chips and
high fructose corn syrup

among other ills
who we really are
is not buried by the pathos
piling up
through the last six hundred years. No
matter that, in this moment,
pity is required
for the fleeting acquaintance

Hurtling toward us is a time
when that wisdom forces its way out
explodes on the surface of earth
violent expulsions
of interdependence
beauty and horror
suffocating bodies
rise and rain back down
as ice spikes that could maim
could just about disfigure the life
we claim to know so well
the spikes may look like destruction
if not for sweaty palms
still grabbing
as they turn it to dripping water
the ways in which
we need each other
another of creation's many
many tricks

Our Holy Days

On goofy wooden statues
icons speak to the public
bordering the rez
giant wooden caricatures
red-skinned men recognizable
to the mass distributed world
even to some of our own
colonized counterparts
that is what an Indian should
and does look like   chiseled
welcoming
buy cigarettes here
get yer cheap vices here
most the time
it occurs to an onlooker

this is not the full story   sometimes not

But someone has just asked
about inside a real reservation
what goes on in there
well, some thoughts
it is a place
where dreams die
and where dreams are changed
and where generations endure
unchanged in their hopes
where you always boil the tap water
for a long time
because who knows

"This is my mom/
this is my mom/
this is my mom"
shouts someone's hyperactive baby

as he punches and thrashes
at a balloon that rises above
and away from him
while he accepts that
hours earlier and again
she has left him
to chase a high, elusive
as those balloons are to him
while he tries with his small body
to influence their wavering

Alone in the kitchen
working on a welcoming supper
for a group of elders on the way
the skittish mind of a childless woman
wanders beyond
immediate tasks—handcrafted sandwiches
cut in shapes designed to amuse
the ones for whom they are made—to make
two quarts of canned tomatoes stretch
to all the mouths that may savor them
even with a bland, familiar taste
opening the second jar
(the water boils
at least twenty minutes)
a motherless baby
tugs at her sleeve, asks why
sweetgrass is kept
in tight, shiny braids
around the house
and why some are unraveled
and why it smells so good when it burns
and where they come from
and if he can have one

In the hurry to keep up
questions echo
finally an opportunity
to answer
to have a captive audience
for all there is to share
about Our ways
but before the answers are spoken
he is gone
the thought started as a prayer
prayer went into cedar
cedar joined the sacred element of fire
thought became smoke
prayer became air
the child breathed in the air
the scent and memory reached him
the way it reaches us each time
and one day, when he can
listen, he will hear
  all that is true
    about the sacred hair
        of our mother, the earth

These babies
with no mother
coil around our ankles
like seahorse tails
the hope is to bring them in
and away
from the dark matter
of the universe
pulling at human weakness
as we venture into life
searching for meaning
connection and love

eternal is the unknown
of the coming times
questions like scents linger
long after minds depart
from the tragedy and tether
of the material world
where trust must be placed
in the energy field
surrounding the earth
and each living thing
as they work for balance

When we are here
and encounter
abandoned souls unraveled
the spirit intervenes
like smoke disintegrating into air
proves
as a people
we were never conquered
unfettered by the sadness
that penetrates this life
the last six hundred years
because we have known all along
while we are in these shells
we can reach to
mold one another
with our earthly time
where each path is lined
with golden strands of holy
and sweet grass
where the same vibration
echoes within each of our bodies
where translating these answers
is the beginning

of a life's work, work
that cannot be done alone

The Penguin Feeding

Tiny beloved
planted within you
are remnants so familiar
little boy whose perfect heart
expands far beyond
the years of jaded strain
infecting those elder to you
at times, but not ever
in our time together:

When we visited our aquarium friends
as promised, we watched them
bite nip and compete
over handfuls of krill corpses
flung to them
from a bucket

Sent, you walked
not two feet away
to a flock of pushy kids
they all wanted their turn
they looked like you
in stature and fashion
little fleece pants
flashing sneakers
t-shirts of cartooned animals
and Kool-aid stains
cheese puff smears.
They, too, were just learning
the nature of animals, confinement
a life defined by wars

Right away you thought
you would need to push your way
to the front

and asked how to make it
through the crowd to the glass
you were told to ask, explain
that you, too, would like to see
the penguins eat
there was no way to know
how the kids would react
a feisty bunch, but moments later
over their small heads
there you were
at the front of the line
the crowd gave way for you

The hope is that this will happen
again and again, as your gentle life
and its curious purposes unfold
as you become the pacifist
unafraid to ask permission and give
before you move forward
before you leap into the sacred unknown

Becoming: A Descendant's Story

> *"the life of a man is a circle from childhood to childhood . . ."*
> HE áKA SáPA (BLACK ELK)

DARKNESS: BEFORE THE BEGINNING

In early adolescence
it seemed hell
was always on the way
conditioned brain thought
in order to reach hell
body would have to die
(untrue)
the mind accepted
popular culture's promise
apocalypse awaits
terror stalks humanity
outer world darkens
hideous mirror
spit back words
pig, demon, ugly hated
everything
eyes rolled
like how teenagers' do
to hear words like
washte and *wakan:*
that which was
beautiful and *sacred*
did not exist
in this life
body equaled vessel
attracting pain
sincere in wanting to die
thought of ways to go
o the humanity

somehow stayed on the earth
a walking cadaver
navigating nothingness
became life/ *"life*
is my possession" said the body
like all creation's gifts
nothing really was
a long silence began

Awakening: Dreams

Late teens the body balloons
to three hundred plus pounds
feeds on feeds feeds feeds
dances at night in sweaty clubs
gravitates to dark places
abuses self permits abuse
from others
cuts skin burns skin
never cries makes scars
pushes hate inside
body feels rejected
mind half-functions
people disappoint
and yet the family
endures body's tantrums
family drags body
to ceremonies to socials gatherings
face sneers at the people
people it comes from
thinks the people
form a procession of absurdity
when they gather
in ridiculous traditions

body remains numb
from bottom of spine to edge of aura
body wakes one day
says enough
says farewell in head
to favorite grandfather
"*the only one who understands*"
doesn't try to explain to anyone
instead
goes to hardware store
buys foam tubing
to plug up car's exhaust
"*the monoxide will do it*"
think the body and mind in tandem
soul nowhere in sight
body gets in car
drives a long way arrives at a deep lake
the tubing does not
plug exhaust pipe as planned
vehicle spits tubing out
once then again
the failure repeats itself
body gets tired of trying
so many rejections
body is fearful to plunge into water
to drown itself
instead says it will take
another day
it will accept another day
it will endure another day
turned into many

Years later a dream
showed the end of life on earth
a blackened sky pulsed with thunder

air shook skittish lightening
violent forces chased body
sky swallowed continents
the last thing to appear
a buffalo skeleton teetering with flame
one other human
was there: a woman a poet
she would not shut up; expelled
supernovas of thought
spoke of love equals life
talked of being good to oneself
was domineering
obnoxious but yeah true
the body the mind the being
hated itself for not being her
in waking
a boy the being tried to love
took sharp stones words like
"fat c——"
"stupid bitch" threw stones
where love tried
to crawl out of body
failure
the pain *"love failed"*
thought the mind
believed the pain
instead of the woman from the dream
saw human interaction
as ill wired circuitry that repelled itself
unchangeable
body tried to drive itself over a bridge
crashed
unscathed
narrowly escaping DWI
a botched demise

once again

In later dreams
the Great Mystery came
with hugs
took the form of a man
a real nondescript kind of guy
in jeans a t-shirt
he held an extended arm
one of stubborn grace
our Creator
pulled the body close
u-turned the mind numerous scenes
all those times
a self
trying to destroy itself
funny faces
semi-enraged dialogue
a cartoonish backdrop of memory
body saw itself saw its dubious sneer
a little child planning dramatic exits
no difference in the face
crying or laughing
it was the same face
under the masks it wears
to survive
next: sudden ineffectual
jerking of head as car crashes
into guardrail
body remains erect
unharmed
the face is stunned annoyed
irritable
fists punch the air
mouth yells *"this is BULLSHIT "*

body and car did not reach
the base of the cliff
they aimed for
instead
both sat rocking back and forth
stuck in such a way
the car would not make it over cliff
and in fact pointed backwards
as if to say:
just drive away
as body and car depart
faint chirping birds and rustling leaves
from soft wind said
all is well in the world
even in the face
of trying something
so horrible
there is no word
in natural language
for it
after the storm of another
suicide
attempt
the body's extremities awakened
to the natural world

In dreams
these pasts were relived
at the urging of the Mystery
we laughed at memories
at self
at the soul nervous
hovering over body
then we went
to a familiar waterfall

called *kitchi kabekong*
by the Anishinaabe
of blood's memory: great falls
where thunder and water mix
the entity pointed
to its deepest part
with his lips
the way the old men do
jump in he said
jump now
laughing
then it seemed
a big wish was granted
the muddy savior came
guiding toward death
beloved
long awaited death
looking forward to it
the body did like he said
jumped
so thankful
the mind thought
as the body leapt
thankful
for no more living
body floated through mist
landed on feet
very much alive
        he did not explain
                just laughed
                        stuck his chin out again
now your turn he said
pointing toward
a group of onlookers
who watched the body

disappear into
and rise
from crooked rocks
jagged sprays of water
the lost soul
diffused from mist
into body
with no questions
the same body
directed the people
how to jump
how to regain
placement for soul
the Great Mystery watched
smiling

That was not the first time
brittle chunks
decaying masses of misery
dropped
like blown dust
to a constantly rotating earth
not the first time
the body's believed emptiness
was replaced
by formless souls
of ancestors
who stepped in
at that misty position
between life and death
laying mud down
for a new nest
a human
who knows
her origin:

Anishinaabekwe
a woman
of the original people
there was one truth
in these survivals
the comedy
of enduring oneself

Onward

Now the body knows
to survive
the mind
must manipulate words
the soul
salutes death
knowing
that transition
will go down
soon enough
the mind works to explain
dreams
to all our relations
the mouth talks
listeners are patient
blessed
they sit through it
while the soul tries
to describe its travels
the body dances
among the people
happy healthy
body holds light in spine
the self the entity moves
to share light

and holds dreams
cherished rough experiences
they permit
a way through life
a way of understanding
of tolerating
of healing
dreams
the soul remembers
the world is composed of mirrors
the body's learned darkness
mirrors of a people lost
mirrors tried to destroy—
and didn't
now
when this entity dreams terror
she recognizes
the invitation
to survive beautifully

Insomniac Receives Prayer

A gift: arcs of morning light
       life has come another day
       eyes bloom open
       air tells stories of the prior night

Elsewhere on the planet
       the ocean sighed
       as waves like hands
       rose to caress the surface
       fragments to survive
       the darkest depths
       rose to a curious shore

Elsewhere soft feathers of an eagle's wings
       folded over fragile skulls
       newborn eagle babies

Elsewhere a tired mother's arms descended
       pulling curtains together for the evening
       while children were subdued into growth
       and deeper breathing patterns;
       the realm of spontaneous healing

Elsewhere are relatives humans dear brothers
       dear sisters some do not despise
       themselves so much that they believe
       we are all, starting with one, worthless

Elsewhere a beloved heart prayed for the misguided
       in the world, the afflicted the pitiful
       present company included
       it had to be this grace
       which allowed burning eyes
       to swoop like pendulums
       toward their way closed

human grace
dismantled a seething brain
those short six hours ago
when it was back there
rummaging through
its known purgatories
masks of karma thought unresolved
futures of obliterated landscape
fire darkness starvation and human
to human violence
a constant practice
grey demolished coral reefs
inert forests
steel machinery and blood
everywhere

Somehow calmness trickled through
layers of debilitation
while punishing fear stabbed
at curves of the skull
acrid waking nightmares melted
in paralysis
under sleep's chemical eclipse
a wave
spontaneous serenity broke the darkness
eyelids sighed closed
brain's frantic activity splattered
to a dull spark
in a moment of light under pulsating stars
that come and
yes go
as certainly as the worst of times

The Human in Tsunami

At dawn she awakes
her skull spins yet is fixed
pulls dreams toward its center
cracks open
like earth's crusted surface
her soul gathers
toward the thick of it
tries to materialize for the day
dust settles mind scans
memories: yesterday
fists beat into dashboard
hurt self no one else
so much pain and
what Is the origin
is it a bad heart
heart has after all
left body
and floats among clouds
as if chased away
by stakes of agony
and it's time to remove the hurt
from the heart
one by one
like fruits
                    whose rooted heart
            lives beneath the soil

Souls are mirrors:
what exists here
                    exists parallel
              so hurt anything
        and the pain exists
parallel in that

Today this body

departed from oneness
and landed nowhere
its center maintains
a roar and a seething
bludgeoned heart rages
senseless as a killer tsunami
one that eliminates thousands
leaves more asking "why, why"
despite what we know of the planet
and its sensitivities
following the storm
a parallel energy arrives; benign
weightless and new
like iridescence in rainbow flecks
on abalone shell, fleeting
to the eye there
flashy one moment
and dull the next
                    the soul too
               sometimes its behavior
        so dark so violent
until brighter colors appear
the dust of the stars the raging ocean
and the self
are the same creature

Wait—the planet's gone
        or was that the dream?
Bad breath, yes
we the people are still here
fractured psyches live
just inside the ribs
        outside a woodpecker
jabs at a sparse pine
then like the tree

it does nothing
a singular onlooker crawls
from the core of an earthy bed
to wake and gaze
upon printed stories
of a war-ravaged world
as if somehow this body
this life this existence was apart
the same wrenched struggle

So We Spoke

One
perceived separation
deficient self-image
thought herself unable
to talk to the water
because words were English
and not
an authentic language

Pushed by fingertips
waves of gritty saltwater
came forward
from distant crashing
to seep between planted toes
(these of a human)

Bubble formations went flat
words arose from the entity
the ocean
it's not how you talk, but
how you listen
permission to let go arrived
as sacred tobacco scattered
from an open hand
impulse said
take some sand with you
but no
the time to take
was no longer

On the bloated surface
scars hold
one contorted face
when it cries
movements are gradual

stories rise to the surface
from beneath the water
against
thousands of years of pressure

Sea foam spoke once again
you have just seen
a good roar
the voice went on
no one is to blame for history
we should say
really
in case you are not devoted
so do not know
of our possibilities

Molting with grace
the wind carried tiny silver
sparks of sea spray
our tears fell easy
both pain and catalyst
saltwater joined saltwater
on a shore that receded
but returned each time
to give again
with each crash
each arrival
the same sorrow

To See With You

Is in fact the dream—outstretched legs
T-bone against a river's bank

careening waves rush to us
with reports of faraway sunlight
through clouds the heat scalds bare skin
and it's that searing
the same thing we see
as we lean
toward the faces of one another
under a boisterous halo of fire
so similar to the light in human eyes
we like the way they match
how sweet the air
as it enters our bodies
soothes us
welcoming when we do
all that any person needs to do: believe
in being part of everything
while knowing
we are attached to nothing
so do we need to break away
and do anything but appreciate
the warmth we feel
in moments of serenity
while above, rising or falling
is constant activity from the same
unwavering star, bringing
shared light our oneness
to splatter across the surface of water
sudden bursts so sharp so bright
for little human eyes
the sun doesn't think of it as work
to burn so hard
at the end of the day it leaves
a scathing hole ducks under
as too we lie here
tiny portals of wavering heat

sinking into earth's rickety terrain
over plush beach towels
reeking of coconut, barbecue
and minds that do not worry

Such a nice dream for us
humans, persons

No Other You

You wanted to know
is there someone like you
to like you
and here's the answer
never did send that postcard
but remembered you
the idea of you
while eating pudding
in little cups
from the convenience store
off the interstate
the ones that don't even
taste good but did at one time
when a starving belly found them
stray in a purse
thinking ooh a snack
it was just after we met
a feeling an association was engulfed
distant knowledge
you had crossed
another path somewhere
but at no known address
no full name
not even an eye color
blind memory oozes
an inveterate place
in the cosmos
when you were there
seen and felt

What would you say
these months later
to the arrival
of such a card, a corny stamp
a picture of Suquamish men

offering to the sun
handwritten reference
to the pudding its plastic taste
creepy lukewarm texture
are you getting this
it's been torment
trying to grasp
at your far-gone presence
in every face that passes by
and isn't yours
the pudding cups are
in this small town
surrounded by conifer
mist in the Olympics
identical ones available at home
mass produced
on sale at the supercenter
a dollar apiece
traveling from a central source
to become
someone's tragic nourishment —
seen them in a care package
for troops in Iraq
seen them being shipped off
to tsunami shaken Japan
jeez everywhere
the species is bathed in destruction
and still there is the savory
in this case a snack pack

Those who believe
there is not enough
say, love—say, food—
those who darken
and yet heal the world

with little storms and fits
you know even we count
in this equation, those of us
who abandon what's known
and run from love
from each other
we too believe
there is not enough
so we hide in flimsy plastics
the momentary sweetness
is not enough-
well it sure doesn't last
but hey
love has different ethers
like we all have different shades
of sepia olive peacock
in our eyes
the desire to be liked or
seen or known
like love like hunger
does not perish

Putting the postcard back
words and thoughts
got so big
sadness grew
from the pen your name
was replaced by words
like a letter—dear, truly
not as nouns or facts
but greetings
because no other words
would do, you are not
the pudding
the sameness

the generic malaise
stretched across the globe
there is no other you

Postcolonial Musing

Like thirst and hunger
like disease and livestock
like tyranny and death
came honeybees
containing potential
to infect and alter
every acre that was claimed
but with such entitlement

(cows, chickens, pigs, horses
and honeybees are
unnatural in America
much like a historically accurate education)

In all corners
we see tense clusters
bees hoard around sticky centers
of tight rounded nests
that the food supply of the entire world
depends on pollination
is a popular belief

This place
they've been calling America
where the world goes
to air its grievances
to bring its burdens
has become quite a creation
a bustling hive that glistens
with silent potential catastrophe
(the setting sun's
pollution clouds are so pretty but please
don't explain them)
if it should happen to realize

many of the things
thought to be needed
thought to be natural
are illusions carried
illusions so charming
but, like the sweetness of honey,
not lasting

The Labels They Say

The label says free
labels declare describe
what is contained within
labels don't mention
eyeless chickens
defenseless genes
seeds cells grains
de-sanctified
in a laboratory
it is a sorry thing
the grey-lined store
it smells of rotisserie
at one time we'd refuse
to walk into this dump
Walmarts or Targets
the two of us said
we'd never stoop to cross
the threshold of the door
or even the parking lot
but here we are
broke lost and hungry
we have come to acceptance yes
we know the struggles
our faraway brothers sisters children
and even ones close by
we know they sweat
break their fingers
agree to disagree
that "the hamburger lives
over in the pasture"
for the availability of cheap meat
on-sale semi organic
fruit juice
which bears the face
of a percentage on its label

declaring it organic certifiably so
the days are love
we wake to the electrification
of a chemically altered sky
clouds of ether razor the skyline
together enclaves of humans
hope for stronger threads
to connect at the level of human
through donations and easy
checkboxes yes send $2
on our behalf but
please no more details
it is sorry
the way oblivion marks
much of what we do
in enclaves nests
where it is okay
the world is in trouble
and still we are thankful
for what we have
there is happiness in not knowing
yet beneath surfaces we've had it wrong
so many years
just under the skin is where identity begins
we too are breaking parts of ourselves
in the globalized cycle
we are stalked by awareness
the depth of hunger
our easy ways to satisfy it
still the questions brim
marked by quick and angry dismissals
yes all is well is here
nothing to be sorry for
no sorry
is there? The label says

nothing was harmed
in the making of this product

Things Overheard

There are those
who walk this life with you
the lines on your palm say so
so how long we been awake now
yes that's we dummy
one is never alone
been a long time it seems
it's clear as your head pivots
on a powder spine
and smiles bounce off faces
when strangers pass by
eyes send forth dull vacancy
legs glide as if floating on wheels
you are exhausted
and to carry or be carried
is no problem but you don't
want to believe any of that—

But maybe if you cry some more today
the bruises in your skull will lighten
maybe if you shatter again today
that salt in your blood will return to the water
maybe if you crumble some more today
the darkness of creation stirs
unformed as of yet within you
the way there is great silence
at the beginning of life and of death
and the start of all endeavors

So yeah maybe if you dismiss
knots of bitterness
shed the studded skin
you call regret
as you spend your days and nights
a slave to the dollars

even as the boy you work with says
it's better to be homeless than to do this
but you need the money you say
and you cry your way through the night
while your dreams bounce back to you
they are the dancing raindrops on asphalt

How can we help you see
in this night, when you leave work so tired
and get on the train to find
everything is steel and halogen
there seems no trace of anything alive
as the train door snaps shut
cars whiz by bearing smeared faces
they too are trapped in this
but the crying is helping you
to slough away the chains you think
keep you stuck in this, remind you
that you are human
and these little storms are necessary
such a thought something like comfort floats
while a chasm of smooth lightening winks
distant in the lowermost strata of night sky
which was once a bed of volcanic ash
which was once sediment
an ocean's floor
which once, in the form of air
bounced to the bottom of a lung
maybe human
and back out again
breath regenerated like glitter
that comfort again right
so you see
the night the sky
know the way of despair

in this universe
it's all erasure and reconfiguration
the way beaming days and
hollow nights
come to gradual ends
and time shifts toward a new face
like yours
a twisted perfection
that puts all the light
and all the dark
right where it needs to be
whenever faces snarl smile
only once do we ask
will you say a little prayer
will you remember
all your relations

Day Of Yes
(International Day of Protest, Seattle, WA October 15, 2011)

They were starved
they were starved though food was everywhere
they were starved though some of their bellies appeared to
    explode
they were starved to know what it felt to be full

They were fed
they were fed ideas
they were fed empty words—freedom, prosperity
they were fed concepts that translated to confusion

They wanted
they wanted to connect
they wanted to look at each other
they wanted to know of others like them
ones who maybe at one time
had families had places to go
had dinners desserts parents
who taught them things
like manners and tradition
other lessons too sad ones
like that everyone has to die at some time
so once they all walked on
he started drinking himself to death in the streets
has been here ever since
but on this day
talking to what some would call strangers
what Anishinaabe call relatives
others who also came from reservation life
he remembers who he really is
he comes sober to talk to be with family
he tells his story
while looking over his shoulder
to hide admitting that sometimes
the streets are lonely

it's hard because he has a weak knee
but no one can know that
or that there are times when he cries
looking into candle-lit rose-petaled restaurants
where fancy dishes are served
on tiny plates with little designer smears
in geometric shapes
and the owners say, you can't piss here
move along

They spoke
they spoke angry words
they spoke truths hundreds of years old
they spoke truths that had been kept from them
the man who spent his life
in faithful camaraderie with office buddies
golf weekends light beer simple pleasures really
a good American life this is what we built together
   isn't it
until hey wait a second what's all this fracking business
he does the research and finds connections
before fracking there was coal and
harnessed water
it's all dirty it's all wrong
how can they cut up the ground like that
soon the earth will look like
a gutted and devoured corn cob he says
he's come to listen to Indigenous women speak
about a different way to look at things
to develop an understanding of natural law
he picked up new information
they had their own languages
they had their own societies
just like that

decades of brainwashing
the results of the American education system
that tell a story of savage Aboriginals
with no humanity creatures who deserve
to be institutionalized and assimilated
undone
and he stands in the streets with his signs
that decry fracking
pamphlets to explain how to fight it
along with spoken comments
about the value of respecting the earth
to look ahead for future generations

They watched
they watched their neighbors
they watched their mirrors remotely
they watched the wordless language of heart
a man's passion died once some time ago
when other efforts at changed failed
failed miserable made things worse really
the brothers and sisters who once huddled together
now stand bitter opposites pointing fingers at one another
all still entrenched in the same system that oppresses
how can one even list the ways in which it oppresses
the intensity of the system's power over
is what brought him the living death he's come to know
but on this day his head looks up his eyes awaken
though it is through the glow of an LCD computer monitor
the effect is incendiary and lasting
he watches his children picking up the same fight
he picked up and put down all those years ago
he watches the cities on all corners of the globe
showing their faces their laments on the world wide web
standing to agree on the fact of something
things so wrong for too long now

as a sort of compensation
certain memories come to life
and he thinks of ultimately action force
creating itself in ways no longer known

They thought
they thought for a long time
they thought of how it should be
they thought about how to look at themselves
spending money is an illusion she says
there is no debt how could there be
when the money doesn't really exist
it's figures inside a computer now
and that is what people have come to know as wealth
so she brings her knowledge she brings her designs
to share with an unknowing world that only sees things
as facts and figures
she remembers that life is a ceremonial healing
back inside the beginning of the world
knowing that her time has come
to bring this perspective
in a world ready to understand itself beyond numbers

They felt
they felt something come
they felt the weight of their sorrow
they felt the sadness lifting and
somewhat unsure of what to expect
they came forward
they came forward to agree
they came forward to warm
they came forward to be with each other

They were supported
they were the support of each other

they were supported by something invisible
they were supported to overcome that which they couldn't
  define
suppose a thought existed
stay here now you might not like this
suppose the creation is tricky, clever
and there is no oppressor
there is no face to match all of the malady
that has come to characterize our divided existences
suppose institutions have been created
to carry out thoughts, to execute maligned beliefs
and tally up human beings
body counts to prove polarity of those
who win and those who lose
but greet death, it is all around
those who say they win eventually die
beneath the sun
beaming on the Puget Sound

They danced
they danced in gratitude
they danced the way all of creation does
they danced for those, their relatives
all living things, extensions of the stars
and the star beings came
to dance on the water
the encourage those who rose up
as well as all those who have died
and will die
in the name of this turmoil toward liberation
and the stars bring with them knowledge
of when the control of the land changed hands
and all that has been destroyed since
the dark side of creation took over
they say like you

we've been here all along
they say like you
we are your neighbors we are your cousins
words like love and freedom
yes all common wants yes
let's share
the ways we define them
and matte eyes
matte skin reignited
incandescent in starlit day
tight energies began to uncoil
during this time when the world
rose up
to lie down and die
inside its own body
no more.

Respect The Fire

The world is on fire he said
the world, your heart, the heat
is taking over. Body is hot he says
knowing of impermanence
you let yourself open
anyway, as a human
it's the warmth and the heat
you go to

So when did things become
cold, was it the cold
that made him turn away
made you turn away
and together you crumbled like ash
that was once a body of flame

So what
if you leave me tomorrow
you'll still be thirsty
he says
pulling rib to rib
under flaming stars we are held under,
held by. News arrives
the Catholics have renounced
former practices, renounced their claim
that anyone unlike them
ceases to be human, so
here we are, humans
trying to be—what? Practical
perhaps, practical
about our unlikely pairing, the certainty
it will smolder, we will disintegrate
along with all things, because they do.
And where is god in all this. Where
is the god that said —

wait, we can't prove
god said anything. Or that
we didn't. So his truth brutal like it is
remains, the world is on fire
plates have shifted
and lava creeps toward everything
certainly it will pour over our union
and for now
unhollow bones hold our weight
as we pass over a spinning globe where
a once-accepted document said by God
all the world belongs to you. Another
incarnation of god says
do what you like,
nobody gets mad at ya. But why
does the fire come why are we left
a pile of ash and smattered civilization
why would you punish us
so-called god, this man wants to know. Why
would you put us here
set apart from those
who own everything
outside this impermanent home
we have built for tonight. Why
can't we accept love
even as it exists so clear it speaks
in this room
through engorged hearts, through
delicate and naked words
these our mere reflections
these our alchemy
and impermanence.
The god we are comfortable acknowledging
says, not my handiwork
you created this, in the grid

in the rigidity
in the structure of your imaginations
you made me this way.
Our dreams overlapped
and in one the boats and the ports
and piers were the first to go up, to start
a world that was burning
vessels reached toward the sky
with red and orange ribbons of fire
turning to wisps of smoke and ash
we hadn't made it anyway
to the light
of day
we lay stuck
with few certainties: this will
all be over, the world is still now
we are so close
there is nothing between us
the fire and its changes
are coming.

Lara Mann

A Song of Ascents and Descents

Patterns capture me—those archetypical, culturally transcendent symbols that connect. The light is in us all. These vignettes of descending and ascending capture a moment, part of its own larger rhythm.

For my family, always.

And for Bernard "Bud" Hirsch, a fellow Illinois alum, and my first mentor.

One of my favorite Bud stories, and some
of the best advice I've ever gotten,
came from when he and his brother were
driving from Chicago to LA on Route 66
in their younger years. They were stopped at a
gas station somewhere in Oklahoma,
and an elderly man said to Bud,
"You know, I've made a lot of mistakes in my life.
And I've enjoyed the hell out of most of them."
Bud was the first person to call me a poet.

I would like to acknowledge, and thank, the tremendous support of LeAnne Howe, whose mentorship and guidance has made this possible. Thank you to my cousin, Keira Mann, for editing my work and for always being a supporter. Thank you also to Michael Madonick, Jeri Doran, Brigit Pegeen Kelly, and again Tyehimba Jess, for fostering wonderful workshops and for their ready, listening ears. Thank you for the unending support of the American Indian Studies department at the University of Illinois, particularly Jodi Byrd, Robert Warrior, Durango Mendoza, and especially LeAnne Howe.

Thank you also to Brian Daldorph, Sally Emmons, Diane Glancy, Dean Rader, John Briggs, Ravi Shankar, Noah Milligan, Layli Long Soldier, and especially Allison Hedge Coke for taking a chance and publishing my work.

I would like to thank, most of all, my parents, Jeanne Mann and John Bryan Mann and Connie Mann, and my family for always encouraging me to pursue my passions and for giving me stories.

LARA MANN

Division of Royalties

When I was 10, I tried to make a pie chart of myself
with no "other," slivered like so many apples
but it never added up
so I've decided to just send it all back:
  I send 1/16 back to Mississippi
  and 1/64 back to North Carolina
  at least half back to England
  and 1/8 of that to Wales
  about 1/4 to France
  1/16 to Spain
  and about 1/8 to Germany
  over 1/4 to Scotland
  and about as much to Ireland.

The phenotypes are all messed up
But I'm not sure what goes where:
  my down-turned eyes to Mississippi?
  Cusp of Carabelli to North Carolina?
  large square teeth to England?
  too-small mandible to Wales?
  full lips to France?
  curves to Spain?
  square jaw to Germany?
  curly auburn hair to Scotland?
  and high forehead to Ireland?

My driver's license lists my eye color as HAZ
  but really they're brown
  or maybe green;
  it's hard to tell,

ringed in blue,
but when I cry
they're all red.

My Ceremony For Taking
summer 2005

No one told me how it should be, these steps
for taking. Some things I know without being told.
The words told to me ended my family,
the words I told burned my family's death scaffold;
those things we say when we are hurt, to hurt.

I wanted to take pieces of my ancestors'
homes with me, the way some homelands are sacred.
The way some carry their birth dirt for protection.
But these locations are revered, and for me,
the taking was blasphemous.

My parents split, and I felt
absolutely halved, though what was left of me
was unclear. I needed a ceremony.
It had to require pain,
a sacrifice. It had to be missed.

That summer, when we went, my dad and I,
back to Alabama and Mississippi
to try to fix our fissured selves.
I pulled out hair many times.

Choctaws were known for hair: long, thick, honor-
banner. I gave of myself. My hair was my thanks:
parts of me pulled out, white-root waving; a lock,
not just a strand, pressed into the dirt I took
for payment, to leave part of myself.

Climbing "Mound A"

Moundville, Alabama, May 2005

In Choctaw, Dad says, *Tuscaloosa is
Black Warrior.* Tusca—Warrior, Loosa—Black.
Tuskahoma is Red Warrior. Homa—Red.
Oklahoma is Red People. Okla—People.
Spelling changes over time, place to place.

Moundville was pre-tribe, pre-Choctaw,
spiritual center city to the Okla:
eye-in-the-hand that we call Orion,
exit and enter point to the Next Place.
Now—State Park.

Our Choctaw tribal enrollment cards get us in
free. We park, walk around the parade grounds.
*Flat top mounds had buildings, houses, temples,
charnel houses,* Dad says in the glowing dusk.
Round top mounds are burial mounds.

This has been one of the worst days for us:
searched at the airport, no hotel reservations,
car time, plane time, car time, and all this heat.
I do what my mom used to do: talk him out of
bad moods; or worse—nothing—just let him seethe.

But this nightfall—Black Warrior River steaming,
radiant lightning bugs, raccoons foraging—
is welcome. We climb the high priest's mound
together, stand side by side at the crest,
watch the sun gloss into the far mounds.

Black Warrior
Moundville, Alabama, May 2005

The Black Warrior creeps heavy, cut in the black dirt.
It flows wide and hipped like an old story,
not like the Washita—angry and flooding,
carrying Indian blood like the hands of
Jackson, washing the red clay dirt down.

We step in up to our ankles, rocks under foot.
The low sun sheens white on the water. *Moundville,*
Dad says, *became the Okla Tannap:*
People from the Other Side (of the River);
one of the three Choctaw tribal divisions.

The mounds heave up behind us on the bank.
Dad and I have come across the Tombigbee,
where the Okla Falaya are from—Long People,
our division; and we have come across the Pearl
where the reservation is, Nanih Waiya is.

My great-grandmother, Pearl, her allotment
is on the Washita in Oklahoma,
used to belong to other Indians.
Black oil chugs out of that red dirt, blood-stained,
my Grandfather told me, from the Trail of Tears.

I would never drink from the Washita—diseased.
But the Black Warrior is clear, clean, cool.
I push a small jar into the Black Warrior.
It fills quickly, I drink a little, top it.
Black dirt swirls and settles.

Shadow World Road
Pearl River, Mississippi, May 2005

Mississippi was Choctaw home before The Trail
of Tears and Sorrow. The name "Nanih Waiya"
is so old, no one knows what it means anymore.
But it is the Mother Mound, Dad says as we walk
the country road, locking in the floodwater.

We go south in the summer for the cicadas
and the heat. It feels old and heavy, rubbing out
those forgiveness-lie stones, swallowed
to make living together able. But our time,
condensed and constant, strains and cracks us.

Where we are is not on a map: squares of green
crossed with numbers but no names, no markers.
This trip may be too late for us but we have to
come home to see. The shadow space between us
has grown thick with secrets, words seep out like swamp gas.

The Shadow World is two things: it is the dark place
in the swamp, where we are now, and it is the place
where the ancestors go. I hold back my shadow
words: affair, divorce, trust, no, man, no.
I hold my stomach hard to keep them in.

The further down this road we go, the trees' thickness
pushes out the light. Something in the tall grass jumps,
ripples the water. I look frantic around each curve
but we've come so far it's longer to go back.
Every surface of my skin sweats.

Nanih Waiya Cave

Pearl River, Mississippi, May 2005

*"A very long time ago the first creation of men was in Nanih Waiya; and
there they were made and there they came forth. [. . .] And the Choctaws
[. . .] came out of Nanih Waiya. And they then sunned themselves on the
earthen rampart and when they got dry, they did not go anywhere but
settled down on this very land and it is the Choctaws' home."*

ISAAC PISTONATUBBEE

A couple miles down this iron-locked road
is low cave in a large mound. Dad throws rocks
inside the gape. We hear shallow water.
He crawls through the opening, flashlight in hand.
I am scared of underground places, can't follow.

There is room for four grown men to stand, he echoes.
I stay where I can see what's around me:
Kudzu-draped trees, old growth, in the shadows.
I can almost see what's inside them, their stories,
but they're tight-lipped and I take my lesson.

Picnic tables, grills, beer cans surround the mound.
Even though it's miles away from any town,
no sign, not on a map, just a numbered
county road, I can see people still come here.
Dad crawls out, throws a burnt log onto the ground.

I want to go inside; shuffle, head down, knees up
into the entrance but can't go any further.
Instead I grab a handful of wet cave-wall dirt,
mossy green, replace it with my hair. I clutch
this dirt-gift, nails in palms, head pulsing heat from pain.

This place he's taken me, this Shadow World,
requires both of us. We had to come
to our Source, go in, come back out renewed.
But I'm not done with this past yet, can't end it
and reemerge; my head is burning in shadow.

Summertime Death Song
Paris, France, July 2005

Billie Holiday sings my death song. I heard her sing for three days in Paris while I lay in bed and looked out the window at the yellow stucco wall four feet away. I don't remember what song she sang. I was not singing to myself in my head; *she* sang *to me*. Dad mixed sport drinks with water, which only made my vomit blue and pink. He had the hotel kitchen make soup, specially, for me. Water came from everywhere. Sometimes I vomited in the shower because I was still using the toilet. I ran out of clean underwear. Dad went to the Innomarche, a French supermarket, and bought me more. He got hit on in the ladies underwear section. By a man.

Dad took care of me. He doctored me for days, making me drink water, eat crackers. Himself a doctor, he called an after-hours house call-doctor, as per socialized medicine. That doctor said there was a virus going around town, gave me a shot for nausea, and Dad paid him in cash. He walked me to the bathroom all hours of the night and day.

On the third day, after using the bathroom, I stood up and heard nothing but my heartbeat. Everything turned shiny bright black. I passed out against the door: my head, falling on my dirty clothes in the only 2 foot square section not covered with porcelain corners. I woke up to Dad's frantic yells and the most pleasantly warm shit in my pants. After I sat up, he opened the door, set me in the shower, cleaned my pants, and handed me a towel with averted eyes. Then we took a taxi to the Right Bank and the American Hospital. From my wheelchair, I vomited but had nothing left and my face went numb. They told me later that was a "vagal response."

My nurse, a woman who would be considered beautiful in France but plain in America, put an IV into the side of my wrist and I received fluids for 15 minutes in triage. They told me later it was actually an hour and a half. My bed was wheeled into a room next to the nurse's station where a black and white movie was showing. Without my glasses, I couldn't see it. When my IV infiltrated, my wrist swelled through the holes in my hospital bracelet and the potassium burned under my skin. Beautiful/Plain Nurse moved my IV to my arm and wrapped my wrist in a large wet piece of gauze that smelled like alcohol and told me not to smoke with it on. Dad called Mom, in the States, to tell her where we were but she already knew something was wrong; it had brought her to her knees.

I was finally able to walk, after three days, and shuffled around dragging my IV-tree in an expository hospital gown and brand new black nylon French underwear. My parade of medical equipment and I went to the bathroom and produced a "stool sample" to go with all my blood. My British doctor, Arthur B—, told Dad that I was a "comely lass," which I thought meant "plain-looking," and he was impressed with my C-Reactive Protein level: 339 mg/L. "Normal" is under 5. He said my body was fighting an infection the caliber of meningitis, but in my gut. He named it "Bacterial Dysentery" and sent us away with antibiotics.

After that, Billie Holiday didn't sing anymore. They told me she was an "auditory hallucination." It's nice to know that, when that time comes for real, I'll go out to her: *one of these mornings, I'm gonna rise up singing. Then I'll spread my wings and take the sky. But 'till that morning, there's nothin' can harm me, with daddy and mammy standing by.*

For Three Days in July the Mid-America All-Indian Center of Wichita Filled With Crystals

On scarf-shrouded tables around the pow-wow arena
            practitioners set up their CD players with drum
    and flute music

signs advertising:
readings
      past life regressions
           handwriting analyses
                energy work
                    chakra alignment
                    and Navajo tacos.
Anything you ever wanted to know about your past, future,
present state, or pasts you didn't know you had,
could be yours for increments of $10.

      I asked the woman with Psy Cards
           about my love life
                and she laid the cards down:
  No.   Death.   Destruction.

Don't worry
        she said
            that's your past.
                For my future she laid down
                    The Stars.

In a past life regression
one woman told me about
    when I was a man in the Renaissance.
        She saw me making a mosaic in a church
while a man stood on a scaffold, painting the ceiling.

In a reading
a woman smiled
    and told me about all the animals and people

waiting for me on the other side. There was
a horse
and lots of butterflies
but these were just the ones who insisted on
being in the front row.
A man, an ancestor, in a sailor suit
tipped his hat, said he was just
checking in.

One woman saw my heart.
She said it was made of
sterling silver
with lacey cutwork
covered in quartz and amethyst.
You've been here since the beginning
she said
Your spirit is a nymph, a water fairy.
People are drawn to it, but
once they get a clear look at you,
you can be gone.

Purebred Hybrid Vigor

I was always concerned with looking Indian enough.
My hair was *too* red, *too* curly, my skin *too* white.
Dad would tell me *it doesn't matter what you looked like,*
it's what you are that's important. But most people
didn't see it that way, especially other Indians.

In college
Dad would tell me
Keep your head down and finish the race.
You're a thoroughbred and they always come
from the back of the pack to win it all.

When my heart was in shreds
I called Mom to make sure I could, in fact,
be loved in this lifetime. She told me
You come from good stock. None of your ancestors
were supposed to survive: first white settlers in the area,
Trail of Tears. You've got their strength.

I don't straighten my hair.
I don't go to tanning salons.
I don't wear colored contacts.
I don't dye all of my hair.
I don't make fry bread, even though I can
and I don't list myself as *only* Indian

because I am
many strains.

A Song of Ascents
and Descents

Save me, O Lord, from lying lips and from deceitful tongues
    the psalmist said; Amen. Amen, Amen. Three times.
        The perfect number, the magic number.
            Holy Trinity. Holy See.
    But not my See, third eye, second chakra, on my
    forehead where I am marked in the Spirit World
as a Soldier of Christ.

Faith of our fathers, holy faith. What were my father's
    faiths? Who did my great-great grandfather pray to?
        Who did he evoke? Hashtali?
            His eye is the sun and his wife the moon children the stars.
        It's not sun-worship,
    it's thanking him for providing food and light
thanking him to his face.

Grandmommy prayed to many: Father, Son, maybe the
    Holy Ghost. Mother Mary, praying for us sinners
        and probably St. Francis of Assisi, her favorite.
            We went to St. Catherine's Cathedral
        where the faithful prayed to St. Catherine's severed
    head dipped in wax, also her finger.
Though I couldn't tell which one.

Did Grandmommy fear Hell, marrying a Methodist?
    But she wasn't born into the Church of Rome
        she was baptized that at school.
            Maybe there's a Johnny-come-lately
        loophole where she and Granddaddy
    can both get to Heaven
even if one eats fish and one eats steak on Friday.

At Sacre-Coeur in Paris, they have Jesus' heart
    as their main attraction and namesake, though,
        didn't He take it with Him when He ascended
            on the third day dressed as a gardener?
        Maybe He handed it down
    like Mother Mary's girdle. *If I have a faith*
that can move mountains but have not love, I am nothing.

But will they always sell me with a kiss for thirty
    pieces of silver? Ten times of three.
        Is that blasphemous to compare?
            Wouldn't that be odd if there was actually a
        Judgment Day where I stand before God
    and weigh against my sins? Wouldn't that be an awful
waste of time? Is that blasphemy?

On Sunday, he said we're all
    saved by the Grace of God anyway;
        no one's good enough,
            there is no checklist.
                —that's reassuring.

I—

　　—will not regret those missed
books, instead
　　—will mourn dirt
not stood in

　　—sleep diagonal
unapologetically
　　—make my travel plans
independently

　　—bike over bumps, smile to
feel my breasts buoy
　　—touch Impressionist paintings
over velvet rope

Straight Line Talking

Do you dance?

> Yes, yes I dance. Ballet, jazz, tap,
> Celtic Riverdance, Classical East Indian . . .

No. I mean, do you *dance*?
Fancy dance, straight dance,
jingle dress, Northern traditional?

> No we don't dance like that.
> Choctaws only dance together.

Do you sweat?

> Actually I sweat quite a lot in the summer.
> My integumentary system is in impeccable shape.

No. I mean, do you *sweat*?
Ceremonially. For the health of your tribe?

> No I've never been invited to do that.
> But I try to eat well. For the health of my tribe.

Are you decolonized?

> Well I wear jeans year-round and speak English but I never
> lived in a colony; I'm from the Midwest.

No. I mean, are you *indigenized*?

> Huh?
> I don't even know what that means.

Have you gone back to the *old ways*?
Are you *sovereign* from the *white man*?

                                Are we talking butter churns here
                                        or woolly mammoths?

After all, traditional is better.

                                      Oh yes, I respect my elders.
                   I know which fork to use at a dinner party
               and stay quiet in large Southern gatherings.

No. Not *that* traditional. I mean *traditional*.
How much blood quantum are you?

                                            Hard to say.
               Are we counting the full-bloods with blue eyes
                                    as full-bloods?

Are you *really* Indian?

                             No one I'm related to is from India.
                                  I don't know about you
                                  but we've been here forever.

How The Great American Indian Novel is Written
after Sherman Alexie

Your protagonist should be downtrodden, poor,
preferably drunk. He should wear blue jeans
and talk about wearing blue jeans.

He must live on a reservation or the poor Indian section
of a large city and refer to it
as the Urban Rez.

His hair should be black.
His eyes should be brown.
If your protagonist is a woman she must dance

at powwows. She must be strong
and have long black hair.
She should have children but no husband.

She should wear blue jeans
and talk about wearing blue jeans.
If your protagonist is a woman, she must evoke power

at a pivotal point. It should be mysterious
and obscurely discussed.
Everyone should be at least part Cherokee.

Your protagonist must struggle with identity
especially if he is a man, and come to a resolution
by the end involving new-found power in his tribalized self.

This is especially effective if he dances at the end
in a traditional way.
Fancy dance is preferred.

If your protagonist is not an alcoholic, a close friend
or family member must be;
see: brother, father, best friend.

Bar scenes must include country-western music and blue jeans.
Everyone must drive either a truck,
a dilapidated car, or a dilapidated truck.

There must be a love triangle.
There may be a maximum of only one white
person in this love triangle.

Everyone else must be Indian and at least part Cherokee.

If a character is named for an ancestor or tribal leader,
s/he must evoke the power of that ancestor
at a critical part of the story.

Ceremonies are preferred but not necessary.
These must also be mysterious
and obscurely discussed.

Animal spirit guides should offer advice.
Any clan-specific animal is acceptable.
Coyote should trick someone.

References must be made to treaties,
government-rationed food, and the BIA.
Everyone must laugh bitterly at this.

Food must be consumed in large quantities
in large gatherings and small quantities in family settings.
A joke should be made about this.

Everyone should call everyone else "cousin."
Except white men.
They should be called "white men."

White men must disgrace
Indian culture at some point,
preferably pan-Indian culture.

White men are not Indians.
But they may try to be couriers of Indian culture.
They must do this inefficiently, showing their ignorance.

Boarding schools must be referenced.
Old ways should be found,
new ways should be reconciled.

Hope should come at the end of the novel
in the form of a baby or an open road,
dark-toned, part Cherokee.

Counting Coup

I.

Before the French called us the Choctaw,
We were the Okla Falaya clan
of the Pan Falaya people:
The Tall People of the Long Hair.
It is rare to find an Indian
with bad hair, especially a Choctaw.
Hair is an honor badge
and to take someone's scalp is
to take their honor,
worth more than their life.

II.

A boy in class asks if
I know how to scalp people.
Yes.
But there's more than one way
to lift a skull cap.

Dad told me how to take a scalp:
If you were in a hurry, you could
grab a lock from the top
and split it in one blow.

Or to be more efficient,
you would make a slit
from temple to temple
above the eyebrows
and rip off the scalp with your hand.

But be careful: skin on the head
hemorrhages from both sides.
Your enemy would bleed to death before
it could be cauterized.

But most importantly: the scalp
and the honor must be worth taking.
I've never found any scalp worth taking,
honor worth taking
especially not this boy's.

Apprentice

The water in our largest pot boils
mason jars, lids, and rims
that I brought up from the basement
as Dad taps his finger
to the Overture of Le Nozze di Figaro
on a tumbler of Jameson.

He stands in front of the mixer
in cargo shorts, knee-high moccasins.
I hand him green tomatoes,
red peppers, green peppers,
chunks of cabbage
and he feeds them
to the shredder
mounted on a bowl
like his Granny did before him.

He says, "Lulu, I remember
my Granny making chow-chow
every September
when they lived in Tishomingo.
This is an old, old family recipe,
except I add honey instead of sugar.
People who don't eat beans
don't know what chow-chow is."

I hold the mason jar with tongs as
he pours the sweet relish in,
twisting the rim little bits at a time
so not to burn his hand.
He puts his arm around my shoulder and
we stand back to look at our work:
a dozen murky quart jars ready
for pintos, black eyes, and cornbread.

He smiles, "How 'bout
next year I hand you the vegetables?"
We listen to the rise and fall of violins.
The lids suck in on themselves
pulled or pushed by
something we can't see.

War Medals

Grandpa doesn't talk about his war medals.
They array his dress uniform
the pinks and greens
in one of the back bedroom closets.
He loves to show his *Ko-rea* slides:
all his company's tanks in a row
shiny with the ten pounds of wax
Grandma sent to impress his superiors,
Marilyn Monroe a purple dot
over a sea of officers in brown,
him standing proud next to his tent
hands on hips.

One evening he handed me his dog tags
to keep safe,
the ones I thought he'd be buried in.
There was a third charm dangling,
a St. Christopher medal,
and on the back it stated:
"I am a Catholic. Please Call a Priest."
I asked Grandpa,
a Deacon at the Methodist church,
about this and he half-smiled:
He was with all of us.

In the Absence of Bone Pickers

In the old days
when a Choctaw died
he was put on a scaffold
for months
until the flesh
came off easily.
The birds would
do their part and
the Bone Pickers the rest.
The bones were collected,
buried, making a small
Mississippian Mound.

Grandpa
a quarter Choctaw
called from Oklahoma
asked how I was doing
"up at that Yankee school."
Said they had to put Duke,
my horse, down
because he was so foundered
he couldn't stand anymore.
Grandpa carried grain to him
for three months
and water
for a week
in the cattle pasture
on the original allotment.
He died there.
But because it was July
no rain for months
they couldn't dig a hole.
They dragged Duke
to the other pasture
on Aunt Annie's land

put him in a grove of trees
let the coyotes do their part.

Months later
when it rained
they dug his hole
had a marker made
engraved in steel
Duke: A Good Welsh Pony.
They found his bones,
mane, tail, hooves,
brought him home
to the original 160
"like the old Choctaws"
Grandpa said.
He didn't know
the ceremonial song
so instead he sang
Swing Low
Sweet Chariot
Coming for to carry me home.

Fourth of July, 1994
Vicksburg, Mississippi

The day had wasted away into
walks around Natchez burial mounds,
fried chicken for a late lunch,
and pictures next to stone
Confederate soldiers.
We bought the official tape of
the final resting place of those who
did and died in Dixie

I sat on a stone bench in the garden
to watch former debutantes
stumble, giggle, and light firecrackers,
suspended in the twilight

The Mississippi wet heat and the sparks
burned the edges of this bell jar place,
vacuous for so long. They cracked
its fire-and-blood casing,
began to slowly decay.

Silver Creek Sound Stage
Clements, Kansas

We were movie stars,
exotic princesses, and pirates
directing dinner theatre
in Grandma's old make-up
and petticoats, aunt's prom dresses,
choreographed to Patsy Cline.

The barn was a walled fortress
the haystack a tall tower,
and jumping off it
was a heroic deed.
We walked the cross-beam plank,
made Tom and Huck hide-outs.

Our hollow movie cameras rusted
away down the creek, caught on
the old headstones
pushed into Silver Creek
when the cemetery was moved to higher ground,
bleeding a ghost brown stain.

Grandma's Yard Art, or,
Morning Mood from the Peer Gynt Suite
Clements, Kansas

Volcanic glass glints
in the dirt
next to a white enamel
bucket speckled
with rust spots
Grandma dropped under
the dripping faucet.
The glass
gathers sun,
sheens it onto
orange day lilies,
overgrown grass sprigs.
Child's-diamond blue,
smoky grey, daffodil
liquid-licked
curves of melted
fire push heat out
onto green. They never
take enough in
to alter that
blaze-birthed surface.

Silver Creek Water Spider, or,
Aase's Death from the Peer Gynt Suite
Clements, Kansas

Indigo haze at dusk.
Marionette lightning
bugs suspend on angel webs.
In rocky shallows water spiders
spread the surface, pushing glides
to prostrate leaves of Silver Creek,
catch on wire barbs.
Our firefly child eyes look
on flickering as
stones in our hands
from darkening heaven
splash the spider's surface,
pushing down
to serrated bottom.

Cousin-Kin Carnival, or,
Anitra's Dance from the Peer Gynt Suite
Clements, Kansas

Little girls twirl and sway
as they know the fairies must,
open eyes wide
to catch ghosts.
Honey tangle of
hair divined in dreams
seeks out the edges
of air. Seeing fingertips
flutter where they may.
Hand in hand they tell
tales of ancestor queens,
of Jane, of Jessie.
Sweet breath whispers
of sacred lullabies
turning stones to dreams.
Carnival waltz
grass trouncing dance:
pas de bourrée et balancé
around the trees in
their kingdom lands.

Silver Creek Fruit and Stock Farm Barn, or,
The Hall of the Mountain King from the Peer Gynt Suite
Clements, Kansas

Slipping through
the half-swung door
outside to in,
mildew beams outstrip air,
molded grain musts out the light.
Bales of hay un-hug themselves,
twines untwisted by time,
but still stair
to the hewn walnut crossbeam.
Near the top a sinking ankle
reveals a black snake's hollow,
a tight fist of angry woken sleep,
and the serpent strikes in a fury.
An off-kilter lunge for the cross-beam
brings peace from the black beast
but the hand-hewn hatchet
jags on the ancient walnut surface
splinter into fleshy fat,
dusty grey in the quickening scarlet.

Affliction of Ritual

If I can keep the two sides balanced: equal touches, numbers same, crack this knuckle and then the other, run into the doorframe on the right, take it back on the left, then the world is at peace. If I fail, I walk crooked, one of my sides is larger, half of my aura dimmer and the damage control to take that back is twice as twice as hard: do it until it feels right again. Repeat.

The most holy and perfect number is three. If things in my world exist in threes then I am calm. The most soothing visual of this is a triangle or three vertical lines. But three doesn't evenly balance well. Two threes are alright but that is six and twelve is much better: four threes, easily halved into two threes. So it's that many times I step every other foot, turn the light on and off, blink my eyes at the sun, pet the same part of the table in the same way. The final time always has a bit more flourish so as to signify the end of the set. And sometimes when I get to twelve, it's still not right. And I have to start again. And again, until it is.

"Sorry" makes things go away, even things that don't necessitate apology. Meaning it doesn't matter but inflection does because the purpose is twofold: the person must feel my sincerity and they must forgive me. Say it three times, completeness. And then again because I annoyed them. And then three times again because the first three became four. But a mere three more makes an even ten (as well as three threes with an alternate, in case one of the sorrys falls along the way).

Even the acid burn embarrassment for knowing better than mad-house logic subsides more quickly than the insatiable need to balance my body with numbers; that need that feels like the inevitable saliva-rush doom that means vomit. The cure is to say a little word and have someone hear it, merge the side-to-side with the one-two-three, knock the other elbow at the same angle, make the tingle spread across and evenly coat, and hope that the usual three or ten or twelve times will pacify.

Ceremony Reclaiming

There're just too many things, too many things, too many things on my dresser in my bedroom and I need to clean so they're not so *there* junking everything up. But I don't want to hurt anything's feelings by being moved. The pictures have to stay because I don't want to disrespect the people in them by being moved. Who I represent represents me. The only way I *can* move them is to move them to a higher place of honor, either a more public place or a higher shelf. Or both. But they have to stay, so I'll just turn them at slightly different angles so as to balance each other. The atmosphere would be too sterile if they were at the same angle. And Mom's grandma's hurricane lamp goes opposite the pictures, again for balance. Around the base of the lamp I'll put three smaller pieces, about two or three inches apart, triangularly: wheat weaving my mother gave me when I went to college, a German blown-glass angel, and a Christmas ornament of the Eiffel Tower. I will pat them each twice and pet them each once to let them know that I still like them. Connecting these two sides of the dresser, with the picture frames at the left and the lamp on the right, is a braid of s weet grass. It can't help but curve and the semi-oval makes the layout harmonious. I don't really know what to do with sweet grass but it smells good and it seems that any unhappy spirits would be warded off by sweet grass. In the center, between the groupings and at the arc of sweet grass goes the centerpiece: a plaster cast of a stele from Moundville. It has two entwined snakes, knotted together at the heads and tails, encircling an Eye In Hand. I don't really know what to do with this either but I know it *should* be here and that it is sacred. I don't pet this much, it might be patronizing. Every now and then it catches a vibration from the wall and makes a high ringing sound. I touch it and it stops. Really, nothing can be removed.

KATERI MENOMINEE

In Tongues

In Tongues is in the rawest place I could take it. It is the visceral gulf between history and imagination.

Veni, Vidi, Vici
—*Julius Caesar*

My hand was on your eye, Father,
void of brightness but still shining black.
Blacker than the iron that flared cold
on your sword, blacker than the thick
of your brow. See how my fingers
made little turrets on your tunic.
I tapped till they bled through your robe,
too tight round your body. When I look back,
I don't see the blackness; I see red.

I was trained to know the grace of sword,
from slender tip to wide shaft.
Every swing of my arm to the blunt of my dagger.
I do not fear the dagger or the numbers of men
lining the horizon like pearls on the shore of Asia.
Pearls so pale they blind my sight. I fear the men
who are at my back, afraid to die.

Once, in battle, I saw my comrade's hand
lying at his side, severed, tendons crawling.
It lay beside him still struggling
to strangle a pirate's neck. His knuckles paddled
oars, every muscle pushing to stay afloat.

Back then, the sea was polluted,
torsos and limbs, floating chests,
weather worn muscles.
Intestines stretched like eels escaping
sea caves. I am not afraid,
but the sight of this made my
stomach heavy on the bow.

I am not immortal but I am the breath of a god,
cooling the ears of my soldiers.
Father, Mars, let their weapons

be blood-bright, their armor dazzling.
I am was not afraid, Father,
until I saw you in the eyes of an elephant
charging, tusks and ivory shining. In the
shields of gladiators, on breastplates, gold
and bronze, your profile was reflected.
Nothing but silver specks of you
that still shone black. I create fear
from grit of skin to tang of blood, the cold
glossing over their faces. In Circus Maximus,
past the stone archways and valleys, the sun bled
reddish orange. From my podium, rays
bounced back across the backsides of
stallions, shone cold from metal off
chariot wheels spinning alone.

Marmoream Relinquo, Quam Latericiam Accepi
—Augustus

> *Those burning ships, their bodies foaming red . . .*

I sit on curule. Thoughts of you brother
capsize my mind, invade my thoughts.
I think of auspicious things: vestal virgins
falling face first up a staircase. On a lake
I see a white flamingo stretching,
its tongue pumping spice into air,
comets crowding, the trail of branding scars
left behind. Garlands uncurling white carnations,
smoke waxing twice and cake crumbs
stale at my feet—untouched.

Dear Brother, I think of your mistress,
see my sister waiting for a kind word from you.
I see you in bed, sheets turning over silk,
a motion, a pushing, my sister still waiting,
your mistress still moaning.

They said you, Marc Antony, loved her skin,
the way her tongue unearthed your chest.
She was more than what you made her out to be.
Her voice, you said, could shatter sphinx;
honeyed wine chiseled her beauty.

I heard you jumped ship with her,
left men dry—scorched meat
on the hull of your vessel.
They stained papyrus,
sewed demonic ink into their soles.
This is why we kept them.

They said she died with you. Her arm
bled venom where the snake latched on.
You fell forward, your sword slipping in

like fingers through silk. Your bowels
spilled out like black snakes searching.
You dragged them down floors where she lay,
stumbled at the arm of her lectus.
You left a scroll of blood streaked on marble.

Your belly erupted, spilt words unspoken in her hands.
They said this, leaving your story half-told,
but I wanted more. That night I dreamt
of how your breath coiled round her arm,
tightening its grip. You screamed, the snake on
her arm burned a language into her skin too erotic
to remember. In my dream, you made temples
tremble when your lips met hers,
the earth felt undeserved and slept.
My sister was at your side, weeping
tears of terracotta, her lashes sweeping dust
from the hills of her cheeks. She sculpted men
from fragments of bone, squeezed them
to powder, watched as her fingers stained mosaics—
tiles of colored glass, of you, distorted.

Oderunt Dum Metuant

—Tiberius

Swim under my legs my fishies, to nibble my thighs, to suck
the age from my body. Blow your youth into my skin for I
want more. Please don't close those eyes; the hurt will only
last a minute. You there, young satyr, help me with this child.
Remove him from that maiden's breast and set him near my
groin, so that he may suckle the milk swimming thick through
me. I will float in these waters so that I may receive all of you.
My toga will open, suck you into this vortex of white water
and foam. Your kneecaps will go untanned, round but still
holding weight, like discus in mid-air. Watching the swing of
your genitals and those breasts that hang the puck of iris will
water this old man's mentula. If I am too old or eccentric to
keep love, take them away. Put them in a boat so I may watch
them rock backwards with the sea. Their memories of me
will keep them full, ward off this hunger that grows when I
see them curl and plume from these waters to wash the gold
from the black curls of their hair.

Vivo!
—*Caligula*

> Blue is the color of your body, and I
> am mounted on top of you—my sister.
> You succumbed to fever or something
> I contracted in my conquests
> of nymphs or young boys. Their stomachs,
> the bend of their buttocks couldn't
> keep me. The veins on your body
> were sunken and drained, nipples
> white, pursed shells on the peaks of
> breasts. Your odor came off deathly
> erotic when it hit my nose. It all came back.

I was three when I saw
my mother in chains,
sent to Capri, where
she and my brother
swallowed bedding—
a sweet asphyxiation
from a shriveled stomach.

At five I tied tiny chariots
to the backs of mice,
threw them against columns
just to watch the blood
paint them pink. Pink
as my mother's cheek.
Pink as my father's prick
before it lost itself inside her.

Twelve, and I had trespassed
over every inch of them,
the elder to the younger,
every trail of blood spilt
from their cunnus, every

orgasm forgotten and
made clumsy in your blood, sister—
and oh, my little centurions.

You were my favorite
and I smelled you everywhere—
underneath my robe, between
the blades of my shoulders
when your thighs struggled
against my head, buried
and unmoved. You told me
secrets that only senators knew.
Whispered tiny traitors in
the pluck of my ear. The year
I became Caesar, you kneeled.
I felt the sweep of your robe,
the bend in your back arch
and dip creating verse with your body.
I knew you earned Panthea.

Twenty-six, and you were gone.
You kept the voices
from returning.

> Jupiter came in thunder beneath my bed, in soft
> huffs of sandals. My mouth expelled foam and I
> convulsed. The guards told me my chest heaved. I
> spoke in riddles, stroked myself in senate. That got
> the senators going. Nothing will make me smile now
> but to see strips of innards, black bowels heaped at
> my feet. I smile when the slough of death overtakes
> their bodies. Or when I hear a senatorial ovation
> before my sword opens their bellies, peeling the skin
> back, and guts spring amber and topaz. Or when I

hold a woman's neck, knowing with one word I can
have it severed, the look of satisfaction frozen on her
face.

If only Rome had but a single neck.

I told you this, whispered
my poetic verse into your ear,
while you slept. Your hair
curled around your face like
eels smoking on brazier stones.
You held back the voices, but
I can still hear yours.
A lyre of melodies, gold
fleeced strings that
remind me of mother.

Remember her screams that
bled from blue canopies, ocher
aqueducts? Your hand against
my face. You never saw the ugly,
thought I was a god because
I believed I was.

Jupiter took her from me. I swatted birds to keep
them from feasting on her body, petrified but still
limber. A voice crawled from under my bed, tickled
my ankle. That night I took a slave not yet ten, was
so deep inside her she split open, a lamb fresh from
cut, red pooling in the cup of my hand. Remember
nothing but—

My hands covered your ears,
your head on my chest.
I made you listen to

my adolescent heartbeat,
like small sandals beating
the earth. My heart kicks
to suffocate the screams.
Forget mother and
her voice soft as silver.

Forget when we were
discovered by grandmother.
But the feel of Incitatus
between your thighs, breasts
swaying with each heave of his hoof.

Keep this.

Remember how your calves shook
when I touched them,
like a steed shaking flies
from his backside.
My hands shook remembrance
from your skin,
corruption
from the thick of your neck.

Efficio Haud Malum Est Bonus
—Claudius

Centurions should have killed me then and there,
plunged a sword through that tapestry
of silk and blood.

They descended on me with a crown
of pinched laurels painted red. I never carried
sins back but left them to dry, dismembered on
those floors,
        those   steps and those   drips,
clouds of brain,
        smoke   lavender
        smoke seared so plum it
            became its own color.

I saw myself in a mirror. I didn't see a man,
but they told me I was,
        and I believed them.

My mother called me her little hydra, so fond
of my face she forgot the features. Her hand
on my cheek, nails clawing to peel the scales
that covered my neck—
shining white jade.
I cheered to forget on the podium,
when a chariot broke bronze on
sand or when a slave was torn in two
                        by lions.

I clap these hands so they don't remember
the tapestry, its lines stretching thin
over the blunt of my nose and those shadows
of hands opening, closing like the jaws of Cerberus.

I see a lion drag a sack of guts through
a mass of sand from a slave, a boy.

His eyes still twitching and belly empty, black.
The crowd applauds,
a howl of hands, and when I stand,

I see fingers pushing the slave's ribs out,
slim hands pulling skin backwards.
My mother coming out clean
in the coliseum, her rotted feet
planted inside his torso,
hair black, streaked with red,
with flecks of glass, bone clear.
I hear her laughter chime. Her hand
reaches out to my face, scratching
          air to grasp me.
I scream and fall back on tapestries.
I feel her hand over my face pinching
the scales above my eye lids. Her laughter
cracks my ears and I feel them burst,

urns full of cremated bodies   overflowing.

I feel these coals black my arms, my lips burn still.
          I cover my ears to
          stop the screams, to
          stop
the stab of her words.

When she called me her little hydra,
I *became* one, men and women between
the crowns of my teeth torn like
broken fig branches. I shed my scales
my stuttering, sank slow to
the bottom of this sea

to sea-beds where pulli may slide them out
with plump fingers.

Their fingers, a forest of muscles, crumbling these scales
like papyri in their hands.

Qualis Artifex Pereo!
—*Nero*

Those flames of Rome, bodies of Christus,
popping like an epic. They prayed to the lesser.

Streets empty from afterglow.

Children crying over bodies, crosses melted
into hide. I see Jupiter on flame after flame,
his tongue slipping and sticking. Its ember
underside, sparking. It laps every burnt rooftop,
the human paste thawing outside the courtyards.
The gushing, the eruption of skin and fat is music.

Their skin melting thick around those
pyres dripping wet music on stones
that hold liquefied organs, broken reeds.

My sound is sweet and might extinguish
the fire sparking on their backs. My people
are burning alive. Their mouths open and
cry kithara. It quarters my side, cleaves
my gut, but my body moves to concerto.

My lyre is dry. It will carry their bleats, their
screams through stone walls. I remember them—
the cream of their organs between the teeth of
wild dogs, tearing singed skin to reveal the brawn
of meat, the melody of veins puckering, singing
to match the beauty of my poems. My instrument
shines tortoise shell and timber, the heat of
hydraulis sounds like throats snapping shut,
my hand twisting around their necks.

My epics will wet their flesh, smother
this symmetry of ash and body.

A silence will rise through Rome
and my voice will break bone.

It will split ruins, build a palace of cruciate stakes, where
my luminaries will shine vibrant on the straps of caligae.

Ego Sumo Meus Miles Militis, Ego Operor Non Sumo Lemma
—*Galba*

When you're near, there is an aching between my thighs,
A swelling. You sit, white toga draping
your body, clinging, revealing every muscle.

This gorge where your waist meets your hips is deep.
I will calm this fever. Like letica on my shoulders,
I will carry you, my feet trudging
shit & piss stained fruit,

So *your* feet will be unsoiled, to a staircase
where my heart beats for yours.
When our feet twine, feet against calf, Dionysus
curves within you.

I'll count every trail, every hollow of skin
to the tip of your staff. You squeeze me—drain me
of my spoiled offering. You told me you were Saturn,
swallowing the bodies of my children, that they would
grow fully in your stomach.

Once when my head was on your chest, I thought
I could hear nails scraping the lining in your stomach.

Think of me as Ampelos drink my body, harvest
with your tongue of thyme and lavender. Our flesh
is made from the stone that paves these roads,
cold lava and granite.

When the sheets turn and twist, our bodies enwrap,
chest against chest. We could mourn the dead or
become them. With denarii on our tongues, Etruria will
paddle his oars through this sweat heavy upon us,
through the trail from navel down to Cerberus
that dwells in the tendrils of your tangled forest.

Per Porro Pipio, Quis Sollicitudo Ego?
—Otho

With me, your absence is necessary,
and the people will grieve in relief,
place two coins to keep your eyes
from escaping.

I dream of my blood. It will pasture this land,
give my men hope. It comes in shapes of flood, tsunami,
in storms where my hand moves lightning, pushing
oceans. The land speaks fertile, and that smell of
water condensing and fruit bearing tells me the storm is over.

There is a field where animals
and birds prey on the dead:

beaks pulling tendons claws tearing the corpse.

All around are ponds of blood and fire.
Sometimes I see myself in a fog, my feet
stepping on shields bent by horseshoes,
blood pooling over every indentation, every
wrinkle in my skin. It draws itself
into the shape of a dagger. I am covered
in arrows, showering me in every direction,
shooting flint through my stola. I see women
dragging their dead babies by a broken leg,
asking me to sew their arms and legs back on.

I will cover this land in a brimstone of silence.

The pugio under my pillow beats, chants a mad oracle.

With me, the earth will not inhale their blood, no,
it will rain just before the storm closes in. With me
no man will die behind you, his blade
glossing red.

I feel the urge again to open my neck, to
feed the earth, a feast any carnivore
would relish. There is a war just outside
the canvas, I can still smell the stench
of death pits and pyres, skeletal bodies
burning on a bed of timber.
When dawn rises and my men's armor
burns in the sun to the sound of daggers
thrusting, turning stomachs
inside-out, the gods will drag
my hand to the crescent pillow,
pull it back, and unsheathe the pugio
from the marble case. I will think about
an unpurged earth, blades midair
in battle, frozen, and the silence
that should have followed.

Somes Mortuus Hostilis Usquequaque Nidor Dulcis
—Vitellius

A month ago, I ordered the public execution
of a girl. Ordered her breasts burned off
by embers. She bit the tip of her tongue,
spat it in my direction.
Her tears made a hissing
sound on hot sand.

Midnight now and still the crowd
comes. Drunkards and madmen
smear grime down my cheeks,
laugh when it drips on my thighs.
A smell even a dog can't distinguish.

The scent of myrrh sizzles out,
the last coal still glowing.
A wet excrement they think I deserve.
They shit in their own hands;
the warmth never left it.

They called me a dog, the ones that run through
palace corridors to senate chambers just to piss
on the white robes of mumbling senators.
I sit upright, grind my bound hands against
crucifix wood, feel the skin shred, peel off, numb.

Children and old men laugh,
the lines around their cheeks
stretching like maps unfolded.
They kick my legs apart,
laugh, take aim

at my priapus. In the distance
a man approaches, dragging a javelin,
tip in sand, the sound is soothing.

But I see what is to happen:

javelin in midair, me
closing my eyes, the
pounding it makes
when it enters my body,
wood splintering,
my eyes rolling backward,
guts drumming, that
plish-plash as blood drips
from my wounds,
pools between sandals.

And me as a child, playing in the river Tibur,
Romulus and Remus floating in a basket,
wolf milk and fur still sticking to their lips.
They speak in images, in landscapes lit
by twilight's shard of sun. It comes in flashes,
my body in the river, my head wrinkled white on a pole,
flowers dousing it, wreaths tossed, and hands
clapping, fingers playing on fingers to rejoice.

And I, with a few moments of strength,
force my lips to smile and laugh along with them.

An Imperator Est Morior Superstes
—*Vespasian*

I told them I won't die on my deathbed,
I will stand, and yes, there will be
dark feces oozing down my legs to
my ankles. Rome has already turned
to shit, as black as mine. Senators crowd me,
whisper things. Sodomy, one says,
poison, disease. The laughter is low but
I can hear it. Littered on my blankets,
it crawls from pillow to ear. Their hands,
cupped, keep secrets washed. Their
contempt is like alms to my stomach.

My people graffitied on walls, showed a
    caricature of me flipping them upside down.
I squeezed them like intestines, thumbs pushing, watching
    the refuge
        that followed. I swallowed enough gold to pave an
empty street, a studded arc.

Outside I can hear gold
flipping in the air, hands
clapping together to catch it.

I stumbled to the balcony,
conscious of not slipping. I
knelt down, felt a pang inside
my bowels and fell backwards.

        I stood up, heard a clash, a clink. I felt heavy
        with child made from gold and silver. Its denarii
        embellished legs pressing against my lungs and
            liver.
        I shake my belly to listen to the bells inside me.
            Those
        engraved faces tumbling around, hearing the

ticks between heart beats. When they sprang out,
in a downpour of taxation and excrement, I awoke.

Rome has already turned to shit,
so what will become of me?

I stand and listen, ears wide
to whispers of mountain breath,
pray that my death may not be slow, that
the pain will last for an hour, the twisting.

I saw chariots on fire, dawn biting her lower lip,
the gods pointing their muscled fingers from flaxen
couches smiling. The gods' laughter. It is all I hear.

Ego No Unus Erroris

—Titus

They called me great, said I had no sin
against my conscience, but what is sin?

Is it the way my arms fell
across my brother's wife,
uneasy with passion around
her boyish curves, or how
my sword sliced open the Jews
from Iudaea. I did honor them, Minerva,
but my campaign was short.

Their perjuries hang off my arms like
folds of hide that slap cold against
my face till they reveal those
who died by my hands.

A Jewish beauty broke bread
with me, but not before I took her neck,
then her body after she stopped breathing.

Juno, erase the mountains of Syria
from memory, those valleys of green
that birthed trees.

Those trees bled once—

The sound of ropes scraping against bark,
toes still twitching, scratching nails on trees
while mothers suffocate their children in their sleep,
their voices cracking through fingers, then
pounding their own heads on slabs of rock or
thrusting a dagger in the cleft between their breasts.

I saw my men beat survivors, push children
into pits of jackals, saw their feet still kicking afterwards.

They threw women in tents to feel the burst of blood
run hot down their cunni.
Jupiter, pinch these flashes of death from my eyes,
too bright to be shown to man.
Bury them with your daughters and sons. But leave
these stories buried beneath my body, wash
my hands in your hair, purified and holy.
Boil these hands until they become bitter
on your tongue, too archaic to swallow
into the beauty of your throat.

Spero Is Est Totus Cruor Postulo
—*Domitian*

Brother, you lie here, fever burning your body.
They said I fed you sea hare, made you swallow
ink and skin, to kill you slowly as the poison takes.
They never mentioned the insect eating your brain,
scratching and clawing for years. Only hammer flat on
  metal
could ease the pounding in your temple.

I don't want to leave you to
your own devices but hear me out.

You were the better.
When Vesuvius erupted
gray snow smothering
the people in an ashen fog,
they burned slow, skin charred
white, encased in a shell.

You were there, sent relief parties
to show them what a man you are.

Then fire broke out, sent a wave
of red which burned streets, melted
rocks piled along palace walls.
For three days and nights, the
city was bright, bright from
burning arms bent over rooftops,
bright with burnt dogs,
their mouths glowing with teeth.

I was behind you, remember?
Deep inside shadow. I was there, Brother,
covered in the mist your cape left behind.
I was never favored by father,
never felt mother's hands rub

my tuft of hair to cradle my head.

I saw you, dear brother, father's
hand on your shoulder, his face
reflected in your armor, from
the hilt of your sword to
the plates on your shoulders.
There was a time I pushed pugio
against your neck while you
dreamed of good deeds.
I never intended to kill you,
but only to watch you flinch,
to press my head beside yours,
to hear that insect crawl, tunneling
through the cavern of your brain.

I had a dream of you brother, dreamt
you planted a seed in my back, your eyes
contracting suns. I hunched to feel my
back split, a golden hump grow,
flourishing from skin.

I heard people chant.
Petals from outstretched hands
opened codex wax, sealing my eyes.
I felt fingers laced in silver, and you,
brother, tapping your head to the beat
of that drum that pounds rhythm
so familiar to you.

Tripp's Adventure In The Underworld
"Marwe's Trial"

I.

Before the Maasai Mara became flattened by tire tracks,
before the zebra tumbled in the fire pit, smoke and
fire cindering their bellies, before the thorns of
acacia felt saints' hands knotting, knew
the forehead of atonement, and the flamingos
popped pink from shrimp in lake beds,

Tripp knew Marwe.

Tripp raised her hands and reached to keep
her friend from falling into the underworld,
into a pit more comforting than her mother's hand
and her father's whip. Marwe jumped to the beyond.

Marwe entered the underworld, and left bejeweled,
her hands and feet dipped in water
glowing with precious stones.

II.

She had the gift of foresight.

Tripp saw this. Marwe took her hand,
saw the journey through fables when
Tripp fell down the meerkat's hole. Marwe
fed her cattle's blood and maize meal,
ground the color of flesh and yellow.

She blessed her and pushed her into a water hole,
wildebeest and waterbuck bowing, blowing
their horns into the dry Sahara.

III.

When Tripp fell, she saw books
tumbling, scriptures written in blood,
baby warthogs struggling to fly up, their
bushwillow branch legs clicking, soaring above her.

A swirl of hooves trotting over wind currents.

And when she reached the bottom,
she saw enkaji patted dry from soil, dark cow dung.
It was the home of the old woman, the one
who gave the foresight to Marwe.

She opened her palms at the sight of Tripp
asked her a question, her cleft
lips rowing her forked teeth:

"Do you prefer the hot or cold?"

Tripp's Sad Tale At The Inari Temple
"Genkuro's Remorseful Rejection"

I.

She never runs through vermillion torii, rather, she
stumbles her geta along damp stones, clanking wood.

A soft mist drips between the torii on
yukata wrapped tight, obi budding blue.

She traces those pillars of red and black,
writes his name in onnade to remember him.

II.

Genkuro is ahead of her, nine white tails
dragging a trail through plum blossoms and boke.

His yukata flows, tails twisting around the wooden mast.
One hand trying to catch him, the other on Tsuzumi,
tethered with his parents' tendons, their hide strapped tight
    around it.

This drum held a woman's shape, small at the waist,
hips and bust wide. She says,

*"When you tap this drum, your mother will cry for you,
and your father will shout storms"*

III.

And when he turns around, she stops,
still as bronze. Genkuro is not one
for goodbyes, feels the urge to brush
his hand over her hair, pull parted strands
behind her ear.

He spins his tail in a cyclone, whipping petals
past her face. And when the flurry of flowers and
snow willow calms, he is gone.

Outside the torii, she hears a crack in sky.
Fireworks like lotus leaves open, leaving
splashes of red, yellow, and blue on her cheeks.

She grabs her yukata, pulls it high,
runs through torii towers whispering,
runs down streets where wind
parts paper lanterns, swaying,
runs past onlookers gazing up in awe,
flashes of color and shadow cut dark
and high on lovers' cheekbones.

Tripp and Her Wolf Noir
"To Snipe A Wolf"

I.

Tripp handed the ammo to Lil' Hood, who
clicked it into a sniper rifle. She wore spandex,
her face buried behind a gas mask. Both
like cranes perched on the palm of a large tree,
branches holding their knees in place.
Hood wrapped her index finger around the
trigger, prayed backwards.

"Your teeth aren't as big as you think they are."

II.

A pack of wolves stampeded through a thicket
of uprooted birch trees, pierced white oak.
When she pressed the trigger, her hands were steady.
Her fingertip felt heavy, and the shock from
the blast pushed her back. The bullet passed through
four wolves. A line of blood spat on trees.
The pack stopped, placed their paws in silence,
licked the fur already wet from blood.

Lil' Hood took the body, flipped it upside down.
She dragged a gutting knife down his stomach,
and what fell from inside him: an old leg
swollen in still-life, neck chunks dissolving
in stomach acid, her grandmother's locket,
melted metal chain, and a scarf.

She burned her grandmother,
what was left of her.

III.

Lil' Hood cooked the wolf, cut blocks of meat to
boil, to stew and burn. She ladled the red broth,
raw flesh, placed it to her tongue.

From tall trees down crumbling mountains,
wolves descended the cliffs. Their howls curled
between their tails. When their teeth showed the moon,
they fell down dead, lying in a pile of leaves
on their backs. Frost and snow collapsed
dry on feather musk fur, a cape colored red.

Tripp's Adventures in Wonderland's Bordello
"Rumple's Poker Face"

I.

Tripp knows she has him. Under Tripp's fan
of cards, Rumple slides a parchment
across the table covered in chips and cards.

With Red Queen in a corset so tight
her breasts are pushed to her neck, she leans in,
fingers pressing on Rumple's disfigured chin.
She bends it sideways, whispers,
"She has a price to pay, and it
skips between her thighs."

Tripp ruffles her skirt down to her knees
and knocks them together. Rumple takes two
clawed fingers and picks a card from his hand.
One flick is all it takes to send it spinning.

An ace of spades, it spins at speed
until it hits the table in a manner
befitting imagination.

II.

Rumple's arms cross under his tunic. He abandons
thoughts of a bad hand. Tripp leans left,

watches a Knave, cigar bent
slightly from the crook of his mouth, slide
tequila bottles and shot glasses down the mahogany bar.

A white rabbit begins to play wild on the broken piano,
white paws on white keys, his pocket watch ticking.

Tweedle Dee with broken feet, limping to customers
with shining teeth and promises of good times
because "it's all been done before."

III.

Tripp glances, she takes a card,
places it face-down and taps her broken fingernail
on the velvet table top. She lays her hand down,
opens her arms without looking.

Caterpillars crawl inside vodka bottles.
Dormouse steals tiny drags from
her cigarette smoldering in a prism ashtray.

Tripp doesn't notice.

Rumple doesn't smile, but breaks his arms
backwards. His legs splinter into sparks of fire.
He dances into a sizzling convulsion till the wood
under him splits open to swallow his limbs,
to suction them down in pieces.

There is a wave of rumors unspoken, hands in silk
gloves cupping close to pointed ears

The only sound: saloon doors swinging, shattering
hallway mirrors leaving glass eyes watching her face
glow between moonlight rays.

Tripp And The Red Light District

"White Lipstick on Red Apple"

I.

Tripp enters without knocking.

She knew it was a cottage of fornication:
karaoke box jammed in the corner,
porridge crawling inside cracks of floorboards,
shingles opening like the mouths of starved
children, water and gutter sewage flooding
over her shoes. Old porn posters hung,
crooked above seven little beds.

II.

It did not smell like a cottage should,
like rotting lavender in bark baskets,
water seeping into a beer barrel.

It was pungent.

You could hear the wood crackling,
a sinister wave of nails climbing
along the cottage, the wood splintering
fingers. Tripp sat at the table, watching
the motion sensor cameras tied to camouflaged
bird houses swinging back and forth,
the rafters creaking along with them.
The red light picked up her movements,
the eye of it catching her heat fluxing red.

III.

Seven little men entered, all dressed in blue
Hawaiian T-shirts, each one had a stash
floating just above his upper lip. Leaning
against anything solid, their elbows
glistening diamond dust, they made
a pass at her. They wanted her to lie in bed, to
"spread 'em wide and spread 'em fast."

They said they made movies, and loved what they did.
Loved to open a virgin, said it was like quartering
a stump with a wood cutter's axe. She looked
around the room, in a dimly lit corner, behind
a wood pile, a thick metal chain
was nailed to the floor, severed fingernails
sticking from a log's opened
sore. Tripp spotted blood-stained
underwear, ripped in two.

IV.

They closed their mouths, licked the
oil collecting on their cubix bones.
Tripp saw handcuffs, sawed-off shotgun
shells, the black coal impressions
left on the wall, and aphrodisiac pills
spilt from a prescription bottle. The men
took a few steps back, readying to pounce.
They wanted to make her feel salted
and stained, like the hobbled deer that always
circled the cottage at night, or the swallows
committing ritual suicide by slamming
their bodies against the window panes.

v.

Tripp stepped back against
a funhouse window. The shutters opened.
She found her moment, lunged out
the window. Mirror glass shattered.
She picked the glass from her skin,
took the trail heading west.
The seven little men stared past the shards,
watched as her image distorted,
slithered down a dirt path, leaving drops
of plexiglass blood behind her.

Biographical Notes

Laura Da'

Laura Da' is a poet and a public school teacher. A lifetime resident of the Pacific Northwest, Da' has studied creative writing at the University of Washington and The Institute of American Indian Arts in Santa Fe, New Mexico. Da' in an enrolled member of the Eastern Shawnee Tribe of Oklahoma and Shawnee history and worldview inform her poetic voice. She has published poems in *Prairie Schooner*, *Hanging Loose*, *The Iowa Review*, and elsewhere. In 2013, she was nominated for a Pushcart Prize. Da' lives near Seattle with her husband and son.

Ungelbah Dávila

Ungelbah Dávila's lineage can be traced back to the outlaws of the American West, the Spanish land grant settlers, and the Ashiihi clan of the Diné. She is a writer, poet, documentarian, photographer and model—she is a queen of all trades who draws inspiration from her own multiculturalism, as well as Americana, honky tonk and the likes of Dwight Yoakam, Lydia Lunch, the Hanks and Vina Delmar. She currently resides in Albuquerque, New Mexico, where she is the editor and publisher of *La Loca Magazine* and creator of *La Loca Linda Pinup-ology*.

Kristi Leora (Miskwadaynz – Painted Turtle)

Kristi Leora (Miskwadaynz-Painted Turtle) is a member of the sovereign Kitigan Zibi Anishinaabeg nation within Quebec and has been published in several genres including fiction, poetry, and creative non-fiction. She is a lifelong dancer and bead-worker, and her creative written work has been used as an educational template for state testing since 2007. Kristi is fluent in the traditions and cosmology of her ancestors while maintaining fluency in the Western paradigm. She has received degrees from Goddard College (MFA-Creative Writing) SUNY Buffalo (BA English) and will complete a MA Environment and Community from Antioch University in June of 2014 with a focus on citizen-engaged water quality improvement.

Lara Mann

Lara Mann is a native of Kansas, an enrolled member of the Choctaw Nation of Oklahoma, and a University of Kansas alumnus. She is of English, Irish, Choctaw, French, German, Scottish, Spanish, Cherokee, Welsh, and Mohawk heritage, descending from Chief Thomas LeFlore as well as Boston martyr Mary Dyer. Mann finished her Master of Fine Arts in Creative Writing in the spring of 2009, from the University of Illinois, Urbana-Champaign. She enjoys dancing, knitting, and Italian Renaissance art. Mann is very proud of her mixed-blood Native and Kansas abolitionist heritage and is intent on preserving her family's oral history for future generations. She has been published in *The Connecticut Review*, *Many Mountains Moving*, and *Sentence Magazine*, anthologized in *Sing: Poetry from the Indigenous Americas*, among others. She teaches at Haskell Indian Nations University in Lawrence, Kansas.

Kateri Menominee

Kateri Menominee (Bay Mills Tribe of Chippewa) received her BFA in Creative Writing from the Institute of American Indian Arts. Her poems have appeared in *Drunken Boat* and in the IAIA Anthologies *Radical Enjambment, Birds and Other Omens*, and *Of Water and Moon*. She has been honored with the Truman Capote Trust Scholarship, the N. Scott Momaday Scholarship, and the IAIA scholarship to the Naropa Summer Program. Menominee is currently attending the MFA in Creative Writing Program at the Institute of American Indian Arts.

Lightning Source UK Ltd.
Milton Keynes UK
UKOW03f2308100914

238390UK00004B/98/P